THE
SOUTH BRANCH
AND
UPPER POTOMAC
RIVERS GUIDE

BRUCE INGRAM

HeadWater
Books

Published by

HEADWATER
BOOKS

Headwater Books
PO Box 202
Boiling Springs, PA 17007
www.headwaterbooks.com

Printed in United States of America

First edition
ISBN: 978-1-934753-27-9

Cover and interior Steven Plummer / SPdesign
Main cover photo by Stephen Brown

10 9 8 7 6 5 4 3 2 1

Library of Congress Control Number: 2014938168

As always, this book is dedicated to the most perfect wife imaginable, Elaine; also to our son, Mark, and our daughter, Sarah, her husband, David, and their son, Sam.

CONTENTS

Part IV The Upper Potomac (Virginia and Maryland)

ACKNOWLEDGMENTS

I WOULD LIKE TO thank Tim Wimer and Doak Harbison who paddled most of the South Branch and upper Potomac with me. I would also like to thank guide Ken Penrod who took Elaine and me on some of our first trips down the upper Potomac and who remains the expert on the waterway, and the Upper Potomac River Manager and Shenandoah Riverkeeper, Brent Walls and Jeff Kelble, respectively, who are the watershed's guardians for the rest of us. I would like to acknowledge the Potomac River Smallmouth Club and its conservation chairman and columnist Herschel Finch whose work I admire very much. I wish every river in the region had a club committed to the waterway's well-being. Why don't other such clubs exist?

Thanks also to John and Arvella Zimmerer of Eagle's Nest Outfitters in Petersburg and Matt Knott and staff of River Riders in Harpers Ferry. John and Arvella gave me advice on how to float the entire South Branch; Matt on the entire Potomac. Both generously shuttled my friends, often Tim Wimer and Doak Harbison, and me numerous times, and the professional staff of both companies was always a joy to work with.

PREFACE

*T*HE *SOUTH BRANCH and Upper Potomac Rivers Guide* is my fourth river guide, following books on the James, New, Shenandoah, and Rappahannock, and my fifth book overall. In this book, I do a few things differently than in the previous For example, in the other works I have worried that I stated the obvious, perhaps too many times—that anglers should, for example, fish above and below Class I rapids. Instead, I have tried in this book to give more anecdotes as I figuratively shepherd readers down these rivers. Hopefully these little stories will add to your reading pleasure and also give a better feel for these waterways.

During high water, every river can be potentially dangerous, and the South Branch of the Potomac and Main Stem are no exception. The most challenging rapid in the South Branch is usually the Class III/IV Chimney Slide, which I have always portaged. When on a trip with Doak Harbison, as we heard the looming roar of Chimney Slide, he asked what was that horrifying sound? I replied that if you can hear a rapid before you see it, that's often a clue that a portage is advisable. Later, Doak and I also portaged a Class II rapid, simply because we had a canoe full of camping gear and saw no need to risk overturning. When in doubt, portage.

The rating system for rapids defines a Class I as having few riffles,

small waves, and few or no obstructions; a Class II as having wide chan-
nels, waves up to three feet, and with some maneuvering required. A
Class III involves high, irregular waves capable of swamping a craft and
with narrow passages or major obstructions requiring complex maneu-
vers. I don't recommend that people run Class IV rapids. And, yes, I
know some whitewater experts can cope with a Class IV—many of them
do so successfully every year, others end up injured or worse.

Another change I have made is that I no longer list fishing and paddling times for each section. On most of the South Branch and Potomac,
as well as on most rivers, a good rule for anglers to follow is to allot one
hour of fishing for each mile of river paddled, though good fishing often
increases the float times. Moving at a relaxed pace, paddlers can typically cover two miles per hour in average water flows, though you must
account for sightseeing, high or low flows, and portaging.

I relish feedback from readers who may contact me through my web-
site at www.bruceingramoutdoors.com. Elaine and I write a weekly blog
for the site and appreciate comments there, as well.

PART I

HEADWATERS

1

THE BARN, THE BEGINNING

O H, THAT BARN's not a myth, it's on Jacob Hevener's farm," replies Gregg Morse, who operates the Highland Inn in Monterey, Virginia. I had asked whether Morse has ever heard of that legendary barn in Highland County where the rainwater that falls off the left side forms the beginnings of the James River and the precipitation that cascades down the other side forms the origins of the Potomac River.

Two weeks later, my wife, Elaine, and I leave the Highland Inn with directions on how to reach Jacob and Carol Hevener's farm, located just a few miles up Route 250 from Monterey in the community of Hightown. Eighty-four-year-old Jacob, short and wiry with a tanned face, greets us at the door, cautioning that he doesn't have long to talk because when the dew dries from the grass he has to "get to work" on his land. Soon his wife, Carol, joins us on the front porch, and they rock together in their swing.

"Our barn splits the raindrops," laughs Carol, as she points to the white barn with a silver roof that lies across Route 250 from their farmhouse, which shares the same colors. Their 1,000-acre mountaintop farm in the Bluegrass Valley rests 3,150 feet above sea level and some 300 miles away from where the James enters the Chesapeake Bay. The Hevener family has farmed this land since the 1790s when they came

Highland trout streams flow not far from the barn where the Potomac River begins.

to America from Germany. On the same site as the 1914 farmhouse, the forebears built a log cabin.

Next, Jacob wants to show me the spring where those raindrops coalesce, so we walk through the pasture on the left side of Route 250. There bubbling up are the headwater rivulets of the James River, little more than a dribble. The James only flows about 30 yards before it is dammed for the first time. "Years ago, we didn't like having a swamp in the pasture, so we dammed it to form this pond," points out Jacob. "Today, the government wouldn't like me doing that. And they would call that swamp a wetland. I like to keep things neat."

Jacob and I return to the house, and there I notice a vintage Blue Ridge Mountain apple tree, a yellow transparent, growing in the front yard, the fruit ripe and falling. Can we have some?

"You must know your apples," nods Carol toward the tree. "Go ahead and take a bushel. Yellow transparents make great apple sauce."

From the Heveners and the right side of the barn, we drive down Route 640 in the Bluegrass Valley, following the beginnings of the Potomac. There we meet Dareld Puffenbarger, who was using a four-wheeler to herd his beef cattle into a paddock.

"Tell Jacob Hevener that my farm, not his, is where the Potomac really begins," grins Dareld. "The springs coming down off his land often go dry in the summer, but my headwater spring never does."

Indeed it doesn't, for Puffenbarger's spring is some 20 yards across and robustly bubbles forth, so much so that this arm of the Potomac, the South Branch, is a stocked trout stream.

"Lately, I've become concerned about the damage my cattle can do," continues Puffenbarger, a man with a face weathered from many hours outdoors, his hightop boots covered with mud and manure.

"I've decided to fence my land to keep the cattle away from the spring and stream. That spring would then clean itself, and the water could even be bottled. With a fence, trees and shrubs would grow up around the stream, protecting it. Even thistle weeds would offer some protection."

I tell Dareld that there are groups such as the Virginia Outdoors Foundation (virginiaoutdoorsfoundation.org) that offer assistance to landowners that want to preserve their rural land and streams. I promise to send him information on the organization.

We take our leave from Dareld Puffenbarger and begin fly fishing for trout in the South Branch of the Potomac. Part way through our sojourn, I decide to jump across the Potomac River. My long held goal success-fully accomplished, Elaine comments that George Washington would merely have thrown a coin across the five-yard-wide stream. A few min-utes later, we see Dareld driving toward us on his four-wheeler.

"There's a bald eagle up the road," he shouts out above the din. "He's just caught something. Come on up and see if you want."

After we leave the Puffenbarger farm and the South Branch, we drive up a gravel road into Lantz Mountain and the George Washington National Forest, searching for other tributaries of the Potomac River. The first mountain rill we come to is too small to fish, but the second, shrouded with great rhododendron, Eastern hemlocks, and red spruce, offers potential. The air smells, well, it smells *green* and *earthy*, as if it comes from an aerosol can, labeled *pine scented*. But this air we are breathing is *real*.

On my fifth cast, I catch a native brook trout, the fish most associated with pristine Blue Ridge Mountain streams and their wildness. The red spots (with their blue borders) on the brookie's sides glisten in the sun. I carefully release the trout back into the water. I tell Elaine that sometime in the next few months or more, the water we are standing in will flow past our nation's capitol and on into the Chesapeake Bay.

That evening, we dine at the Highland Inn, a three-story Victorian built in 1904 as a mountain hotel for tourists desiring to escape the summer heat or city life—easily accomplished as this mountaintop town of Monterey is the largest one in Highland County with a population of just over 200. Antiques and collectibles decorate each of the 18 rooms.

It's Wednesday and that means buffet night—chicken buttiker, Salisbury steak, and pork loin serve as the entrees while lima beans, corn, mashed potatoes, and snap peas with mushrooms are among the vegetables. For dessert, we select the key lime and tollhouse pies, although the chocolate chess and maple pecan pies tempt us. Later, we talk to Gregg Morse.

"Even now, this area is remote—one-third of Highland County is national forest and you have to cross four mountain ranges to arrive here," says Gregg. "My wife, Deborah, and I came here to operate the inn in 2002 as a lifestyle decision, not as a get-rich-quick thing."

Large family farms dominate the Highland County landscape, but Gregg worries that older men operate many of them. Jacob Hevener, for example, is the last surviving male of his family.

After a continental breakfast the next morning and a tour of Monterey's craft and antique shops, as well as the general store, we head home with a better understanding of the importance of the Blue Ridge's headwater streams, and the people who live along them.

2

PEOPLE, PLACES, AND PAST OF THE UPPER POTOMAC

O DYSSEUS VENTURED FORTH on one, so did Huck Finn and Jim, as did my fellow school teacher friend Tim Wimer and I. What all these people embarked upon was a voyage of discovery, in our case the people, places, and past of the Upper Potomac from Indian Rock 4½ miles above the confluence of its North and South Branches to 53 miles downstream at Berkeley Springs.

DAY ONE: INDIAN ROCK TO PAW PAW (13½ MILES)

Although the 4½-mile section from Indian Rock on the South Branch to the confluence with the North Branch has much to recommend it, for Tim and me, the excursion really began when we arrived at the commingling of the North and South Branches of the Potomac. Every time I come to where any great American river begins, I can't help but think about the Native Americans who once walked along or paddled these waterways.

In the case of this part of the Potomac, the Mound Builders arrived first of all; one can still view a trademark mound in Romney. John Douglass, editor of the *Morgan Messenger*, has extensively studied the area's history. He says that the Susquehannocks, who were Hurons,

The South Branch Potomac flows through wild country. View of the river near South Branch Depot, West Virginia.

dwelled in this area, but disease and Iroquois tribes from the north virtually wiped them out.

The Shawnees were the primary tribe in this area during the Historic Period, and their allies, the Delaware, lived in the region, too, says Douglass. Both were enemies of the Iroquois. By 1757–8 and the end of the French and Indian War, no Indians remained.

This area, especially what is now Interstate 81, was a major Indian trail and brought many tribes engaged in war. Killbuck was a Shawnee chief who raided Great Cacapon in 1755. Shingas was a Delaware chief with whom George Washington negotiated says Douglass.

Matt Knott, who operates River Riders in Harpers Ferry, has paddled the entire West Virginia section of the Potomac: "The Potomac from the confluence to Berkeley Springs is the most remote section of the river," he says. "The banks are heavily wooded, homes are few and far between, and wildlife is everywhere: deer, turkeys, herons, wood ducks, geese, and other waterfowl. Although the region is isolated, the river lacks major rapids, mostly just a few Class Is under normal water conditions. Still, few people float this section because of its isolation."

The Upper Potomac did experience a period when the region boomed with commerce. In 1836, construction on the Paw Paw Tunnel began as the final link of the Chesapeake and Ohio Canal between Georgetown and Cumberland, Maryland. The tunnel was seen as an alternative to traveling through the river's Paw Paw Bends, a 6-mile section that snakes through the surrounding countryside. Many area West Virginians welcomed the canal for the jobs it brought.

C&O officials predicted that the mile-long, brick-lined tunnel would be completed by 1838 and cost some $33,500.00. Instead, the act of burrowing through the surrounding mountainside lasted until 1850, cost over $600,000, and was beset with violence.

It is said that history has a way of repeating itself, and the mid-19th century was a time when the presence of immigrants in America was controversial, not unlike today. The C&O hired Irish immigrants for a pittance but then found that they lacked the skills necessary for tunneling and stonework. This resulted in officials importing miners from England and Wales and stonemasons of German descent.

The various ethnic groups did not mesh well; many of those who had arrived first felt the newcomers would take their jobs. When the company fell two months behind in pay, riots broke out. And in 1839, more trouble brewed when Irishmen vandalized an English and Dutch camp. Add in outbreaks of cholera and other diseases, and it's no wonder that the Paw Paw Tunnel did not open until 1850.

Tim and I arrived at the Paw Paw ramp at 6:40 on a Wednesday evening; our paddling pace quickened by an approaching mid June thunderstorm. As a result, we covered the 13½ miles from Indian Rock in a little over 6½ hours. The town is named for the tree of the same name, which produces a fruit that features a custard-like consistency and a banana-like taste. I like to gather paw paws when I hunt in October. A walk of a few hundred yards took us from the ramp to Grandma's.

Kelly Adams formerly owned the Heritage Trail B&B and Grandma's

Country Kitchen Restaurant-Inn, which has since closed, and he is the third generation of his family to live in Paw Paw.

"There's no other place where I would rather raise my children than Paw Paw," he told me. "This community is one of the few places where I've been that a parent can allow children to walk and bicycle down streets and alleys and not have to worry about them. The neighbors here will also keep a look out for the children of everyone. I would like to see my kids and the other children here receive a college education and return to Paw Paw to live. That's one reason why I like to promote this area."

While eating dinner (I had the chicken salad and baked potato, but the homemade blueberry pie was truly the highlight), a couple, Tim and Tina Waugh, in the adjacent booth heard Wimer and me discussing how to transport him to the Paw Paw Tunnel Campground, for that was where he would camp while I stayed at Grandma's.

Graciously, the Waughs volunteered to drive Weimer to the campground—typical of the hospitality we found in the community. Tim Waugh was born and raised in Paw Paw whereas Tina grew up there. I asked them what was the best thing about this locale?

"Well, Paw Paw is a small town where everybody knows each other and gets along," said Tim. "But the best thing would have to be Paw Paw Elementary and High School."

"Oh, yes," added Tina. "The school is what binds this community together. Just about everybody goes to the sporting events, whether they have a child at the school or not."

The Waughs said that each of the school's 13 grades averages having between 20 and 30 children. Tim said that his class (1997) had about 15 graduates; Tina's (1996) contained some 30.

DAY TWO: PAW PAW TO ORLEANS CROSS ROADS (22 MILES)

Near the end of Day Two, we paddled into what was once Orleans Cross Roads, a long trek of 22 miles downstream from Paw Paw—an exercise in paddling willpower that took us 8½ hours. Sadly, nothing remains of the town except a few scattered buildings. (On river left, Fifteenmile Creek Campground marks the area.) John Douglass is part of a family that has lived in this area for 200 years. He believes the community is not named for Louisiana's Big Easy. Instead, the available evidence suggests that Orleans Cross Roads received its designation from a fur trader who was homesick for his French homeland city of Orleans.

During the construction of the C&O Canal, hostility among the various emigrant groups sometimes occurred.

"The skirmishes were often between Irish laborers and others, possibly Germans, though later along the railroad, a lot of laborers were Italian," says Douglass. "In the early 20th century, there was even an Italian language school in nearby Doe Gully. There was also occasional animosity between West Virginia railroad workers and Maryland canal workers, like the cattlemen and the sheepherders of the Old West. No bridge existed between Orleans Cross Roads and Little Orleans, Maryland, which lies directly across the river, until the early 20th century construction of the Western Maryland Railroad."

"Still," continues Douglas, "a few of my Doe Gully ancestors were baptized at St. Patrick's Catholic Church, built by Irish and possibly Italian workers in Little Orleans in the mid-19th century. They would boat across the Potomac or possibly ford the river at low water seasons. The ford was wiped out when the terrain was changed by floods in the 1920s and 1930s, according to my grandfather."

After Tim Wimer and I left what was once Orleans Station near the end of Day II, we paddled another 3½ miles until we found a campsite on the C&O Canal. There, after dinner and sunset, we listened to the nostalgic sounds of trains traveling along the West Virginia shoreline on the old B&O tracks, as well as, on the same bank, a bullfrog that serenaded us. Apparently, the male amphibian never did attract a mate as his guttural rumblings continued until sunrise—sounds that I found soothing and sleep inspiring.

Day Three: Berkeley Springs: Orleans Cross Roads to Berkeley Springs (17½ miles)

The next morning at 7:30, we began our 14-mile ramble to the Route 522 bridge and Berkeley Springs. As a birdwatcher, highlights for me included seeing two bald eagles and a half dozen or so ospreys, as well as green herons, orchard orioles, redstarts, wood thrushes, yellow warblers, pileated woodpeckers, Eastern kingbirds, and a host of other species—some 40 in all. Between us, Tim and I caught some 50 smallmouth bass and sunfish, although only one smallie reached 12 inches.

Tim and I arrived around 2:15 p.m. at the Route 522 bridge near Berkeley Springs where River Riders picked us up. George Washington beat us to the Morgan County community of about 650 by some 250-plus years, first visiting as a 16-year-old survey party member in 1748. Later because of the supposed restorative powers of the springs, the locale would become known as Bath in 1776 when the Virginia Legislature formed the town. In the early 1750s, it was referred to as Warm Springs.

In the 1777 survey, town fathers set aside less than four acres of the springs for "suffering humanity," and that plot (with a few small additions over the centuries) eventually became known as West Virginia's first state park, Berkeley Springs State Park. The town itself did not become known as Berkeley Springs until a name change was deemed necessary because of confusion with Virginia's Bath County.

The springs were known as Berkeley Springs once Berkeley County was formed in 1772. It became the official postal address in 1802 and remains so today although the official municipality remains Bath as set by the legislature in 1776.

Berkeley Springs itself was perhaps named for Norborne Berkeley, also known as Lord Botetourt. Berkeley arrived in late October of 1768 and tried compromise to alleviate the rapidly growing tensions between colonialists and the crown. Of course, Berkeley's attempts at moderation failed, and the Revolutionary War broke out.

Jeanne Mozier, vice president of Travel Berkeley Springs, is a true history aficionado and obviously enchanted with her community.

"The most unique historical quality of this area is that it has been a place for almost 300 years for people to come take the waters and heal themselves," she says. "When George Washington arrived here in 1748, he described the area as 'ye famed warm springs,' so even then this was a significant and unusual place, and had been for some time."

Mozier adds that the only reason Berkeley Springs is 6 miles from the banks of the Potomac is the presence of the springs. All other "river towns" lie right on the banks. The town, she says, was created as a way to provide lodging for folks who visited the springs. Mozier even calls this legislative intent "the first economic development project in the region."

A second important quality of Berkeley Spring is that it was—and is— the gateway west. "Our location made us a sign point for settlers on their way west," continues Mozier. "That was significant in Washington's time and is still significant today. In the 1700s, Berkeley Springs, along with Harpers Ferry, Shepherdstown, Martinsburg, and Charles Town, were the centers of life in this region. And they still are today."

Mozier says that there is no credible evidence of a permanent Indian settlement around the springs, but the Native Americans definitely had a presence in the surrounding area. Arrowheads can be found everywhere in the area, and settlements existed at the confluence of the Cacapon with the Potomac and at what is today the Route 522 Bridge. Evidence from Washington's writings suggests that the Indians used nearby Warm Springs Mountain as a war base.

A PERFECT ENDING

Famished from our long excursion, Wimer and I joined Mozier for dinner at Tari's Diner. There we met Tari Hampe-Deneen, who has since retired from the restaurant.

"I've been fortunate to be able to live in Berkeley Springs since I was 12," Tari told us. "People here are wonderful, and although it sounds like a cliché, this is a small town that is like one big happy family. The businesses are locally owned, and when you walk into a store, there is the actual owner to greet and help you."

As a seafood enthusiast, I opted for the Cedar Planked Salmon, baked potato, and a vegetable medley. After dinner, I walked next door to the Star Theatre. According to co-owner Jeanne Mozier, the building's décor is circa 1947. And, indeed, the red upholstered seats, the old fashioned popcorn machine (a 1949 model Manley), the neon and flashing lights reminded me of the movie theatres I visited as a child in the 1950s. For the budget conscious, the ancient cash register's top price is $9.99, insuring that an evening out can only be so expensive.

Afterwards, I spent the night at the Manor Inn in Berkeley Springs. Ellen Lewis, along with her husband Wesley, operates the B&B and has done so since April of 2002.

"What first attracted us to Berkeley Springs were the hiking trails at Cacapon Resort State Park and Coolfront Resort," Ellen told me. "Wesley and I just love walking the mountain trails."

On one of the Lewis' hiking expeditions, the couple, then living in Frederick, Maryland, noticed that the Manor Inn was for sale by then owner Don Trask. Ellen and Wesley were eager to start what she calls "the second stage of their lives." And she, having been raised by a father in the hospitality business, felt that running a B&B would be a natural progression. Not surprisingly, once Ellen and Wesley purchased the establishment, her father cheerfully helped them renovate it.

"There were many things that attracted us to the Manor, but we especially liked the wide, spacious porch that covers the entire front and one side," reveals Ellen. "When we started meeting the unpretentious folks around Berkeley Springs, well, the move was an easy one."

Ellen says that on the first day the inn reopened, she managed to lodge a splinter in a finger. "Arkie and Alma Willey from down the street found out about my splinter, brought over a first aid kit, and bandaged my finger," marvels Ellen. "People here will do anything for you."

Ellen serves a variety of breakfasts, and I chose the seven-grain hot cereal, which is cooked in a crock pot overnight and served with various fruits. Well-fueled from a hearty meal, Tim and I headed home, but not before we discussed plans to visit more of the river towns along the Potomac.

3

POTOMAC RIVER SYSTEM TROUT FISHING

A PERSON CAN ONLY stand so much, and I had had my fill. Friend Kurt Alderson and I had made our second trip of the year to fish the headwaters of the South Branch of the Potomac. As we had in April, and now again in July, Kurt and I had driven to Pendleton County to take advantage of the trout action along Route 220.

I had graciously—and foolishly as matters evolved—told my buddy that he could have first crack at the pool. My plan was to snap some scenic shots of Kurt fishing and then later, hopefully, take more pictures of him with a fish or two. Back in early April, I had watched him catch and release a half-dozen or so wild, stream-born rainbows, plus a brook trout that topped 14 inches, from the pool. And surely he couldn't duplicate that feat again. After all, it was the first week of July.

But once more, Alderson was battling trout on just about every cast. He had landed and released eight or nine rainbows, and I still had not made a cast, although I had taken a few pictures. But when Kurt caught a 14-inch brown my patience gave out. I announced that the photo shoot was over and that I was going to fish for a while. And by the way what fly are you using?

"Size 14 Elk-hair Caddis," he grinned. "Want one?"

Yes, I did want one and a minute or so later, I too was playing a wild

The author with a wild rainbow that he caught from the upper South Branch.

rainbow. In twenty minutes or so of fishing, I caught six stream born rainbows from the same pool with the biggest trout measuring seven inches. Only then did we move on upstream to continue our exploration of the South Branch.

NATIVE BROOKIES

I have made a number of trips to the headwaters of the Potomac to explore the native brook trout fisheries in the South Branch and North Fork of the South Branch. Interestingly, the status of the native brookie has been the topic of much discussion. Trout Unlimited has issued a report, *Eastern Brook Trout: Status and Threats*, that details the problems that the species is having.

Historically, brook trout lived from Maine to northern Georgia, but habitat loss and land use changes have resulted in isolated populations, often restricted to the headwaters of high elevation streams. In the

Potomac system, that would mean counties such as Pendleton and Hardy in West Virginia and Highland in Virginia, specifically those parts of the stream that flow through the George Washington and Jefferson National Forest. Also, the Monongahela National Forest, in counties such as Grant, tributary streams of the Potomac Watershed contain natives.

However, both brook trout habitat and fish numbers have been decreasing not only in the two Virginias but also throughout the region. The fear among many anglers is that public land will become the last stronghold of the brook trout, particularly in states such as Maryland and Virginia, which are developing rapidly. For more information on the status of the brook trout, contact Trout Unlimited at www.tu.org.

A positive step being taken is the Trees for Trout concept of MeadWestvaco. For years, fisheries biologists and foresters have strived to keep debris out of trout streams. But research of MeadWestvaco at the company's Wildlife and Ecosystem Research Forest, an 8,400-acre tract near Elkins, has indicated that brookies may benefit when downed trees fall—or are strategically placed—in highland rills.

However, this research also indicates that other factors may well come into play such as the quality and quantity of available food. MeadWestvaco conducted more research, placing woody debris in eight streams at the research forest and in nearby creeks. Interestingly, the company opened the canopy in places along the streams. Doing so may make the streams warmer, more fertile, and more suitable for trout to grow.

Of course, cutting too much of a riparian zone can have a negative effect on brook trout, as the water will warm too much. MeadWestvaco will monitor these streams over the years. Fans of the West Virginia brook trout will no doubt be interested in the results of the project. For more information about the research forest, consult http://www.mwerf.org/.

During my three excursions for native brookies, I have experienced the highs and lows of exploring new trout water. For example, on my first trip, I drove through the mountains of the George Washington National Forest for miles, occasionally stopping at the bridges that span the public land's creeks.

After pausing at several creeks that were too small to host trout, I finally came to one that looked promising. Deciding to gamble that the creek might hold larger fish, I opted for a size 8 grasshopper imitation. That decision was rewarded when an 8-inch brook trout sipped in the fake. Of all the fish I caught that year, this one was the most rewarding and cherished.

However on my outing with Kurt Alderson, we too decided to go exploring. After we left the South Fork and Route 220 behind, we drove across Pendleton County to the North Fork of the South Branch. Once there, we made two forays into the national forest in search of wild brookie water.

On the first one, after parking our vehicle and trekking into the George Washington National Forest, we came across two streams and followed both of them for a considerable distance upstream. However, neither one had the depth to harbor natives, and we retreated back to the vehicle. Kurt and I also were a little worse for wear as we were covered with mosquito bites and scratches from our off-road experience.

We then debarked in the car for another round of exploration. Driving up and down national forest roads—with a *West Virginia Atlas & Gazetteer* in tow, we never did encounter a stream that looked big enough to support trout. At one point, we speculated that we had left Pendleton County, West Virginia, and blundered into Highland County, Virginia.

This leads to three relevant points. First, don't expect to find state or county line signs on some of these dirt/gravel back roads. I always obtain both West Virginia and Virginia fishing licenses—a good idea for anyone who wants to explore the native brook trout fisheries in the Potomac system.

Second, one of the true joys concerning the outdoor experience is to venture forth and explore the outdoor world. No doubt, some of these trips will end in failure, that is, failure in terms of finding fishable water. But the exhilaration of locating a hidden trout stream, one that sports wild, brightly hued brook trout, is indeed a special feeling. Kurt and I weren't terribly disappointed that we did not find a hidden brookie haunt. We enjoyed just "getting out" and plan to return to the North Fork of the South Branch watershed and resume our exploration. Who knows what we will encounter.

Third, another thrill that can be experienced is meeting local folks that live along these streams. For instance, Kurt and I stopped at a farmhouse along the North Fork and asked for directions. The lady of the house and her mother invited us in for some cool, well water and even offered snacks.

After chatting with us for a little longer, the two women granted us permission to fish the trout stream that runs through their backyard. They even told us about their family history in Pendleton County and showed us some Civil War artifacts. Interestingly, neither one could remember which side the family had fought on during the war. As many readers no doubt know, this part of West Virginia had passionate followers of the North and South during the Civil War.

Of course, not every farm family will grant you, or us, so warmly. But I have found that many West Virginia folks respond warmly to polite requests for information and even for fishing permission.

SOUTH BRANCH TROUT

Sportsmen have three options when exploring the South Branch of the Potomac's trout waters. One of the aspects that I like best is that all three offer entirely different fishing. The first is the Franklin section in Pendleton County, which is named for the community of Franklin, a picturesque small town with Route 220 running through it. This is largely a stocked trout fishery with releases taking place in the winter, spring, and fall. The second option is to wade fish or canoe the Smoke Hole section in Pendleton County. The trout are released on the same schedule as the Franklin section, but what is unique about the Smoke Hole is that it one of the few places that I have float fished where I can catch both trout and smallmouths. The third option is the catch-and-release area, which is a mile-long section beginning 2 miles below Route 220 at Eagle Rock and extending downstream.

THE FRANKLIN SECTION

This is section comes under the W-F designation. That means it is stocked once in January, twice in February, once each week from March through May, and once each week the second and third weeks of October. This section is stocked with rainbows, browns, and brookies from the Virginia line downstream past Franklin.

As noted earlier, Route 220 parallels much of this section and provides considerable access. In places where public access does not exist, anglers should seek to gain landowner permission. This is especially true when the stream winds away from 220. For instance on both of Kurt's and my trips, we stopped in at farmhouses and asked permission to go down to the river to fish. Over the years, I have found such a request is often granted.

I also believe that the best fishing will be found on the back roads that lead off from Route 220. Yes, some satisfying fishing can be found next to this major highway. But driving along the back roads that lead off from Route 220 or gaining permission to walk or drive the farm lanes that lead away from the highway will often produce better trout action.

THE SMOKE HOLE SECTION

This portion also falls under the winter, spring, and fall classification and is stocked from past Franklin all the way to the Grant County line. This section can be reached via USFS Route 74 or West Virginia Secondary Route 2. You can access the latter near Upper Tract, which lies on Route 220.

Over the years, I have canoed through the Smoke Hole on a number of occasions. The Smoke Hole is one of the few places in the East where anglers can fish for both trout and smallmouths from a canoe or kayak.

The upper Smoke Hole contains a number of dangerous rapids—some with Class III or more drops—that can easily flip a canoe. One of the worst rapids in this section is the Class III to IV Chimney Slide Rapid. I strongly recommend portaging Chimney Slide and other similar rapids. I also must confess that I have overturned in Chimney Slide, in the late 1980s. I was on the water in the early summer, and I don't wish this type of experience on anyone.

If you decide to float the Smoke Hole, commit two to three days to the undertaking. The standard trip is from Big Bend in Pendleton County to Vernon Welton Park in Petersburg in Grant County, a distance of 23 miles. This is true wilderness floating, and you will need to have camping gear. For guided trips, current stream and fishing conditions, and canoe and kayak rental, contact Eagle's Nest Outfitters, (304) 257-2393.

THE CATCH-AND-RELEASE SECTION

The mile-long C&R section begins 2 miles below Route 220 at Eagle Rock and extends downstream. Access is by County Route 2. In this section, only artificial lures and flies are permitted and multiple hook lures must have barbless hooks. Single hook lures may have barbs. All trout caught must be immediately released. The stocking period varies. This section is popular with fly fishermen and understandably so given the quality action.

NORTH FORK OF THE SOUTH BRANCH TROUT

As noted earlier, Alderson and I explored the upper reaches of the North Fork of the South Branch last July. The upper river (Pendleton County), and it is really nothing more than a mountain and highland valley rill through here, contains native brook trout, plus stocked trout that have wandered upstream, especially browns.

The North Fork also offers a catch-and-release section in Pendleton County. This portion runs for ¾ of a mile, beginning at the mouth of Seneca Creek near Seneca Rocks. Access is by Secondary Route 28/3 at junction of Routes 28 and 33 at Mouth of Seneca. This section is stocked in the spring. I have plied the water there several times and every time have caught fish, although they are not pushovers as the catch-and-release designation generates some fishing pressure.

The second section of the North Fork is stocked from Judy Gap downstream to ½ mile above the junction of the South Branch near Cabins in Grant Count. Route 28 parallels this section, which falls under the W/F classification. This part of the river offers standard put-and-take trout fishing.

TIPS AND TACTICS

Kurt Alderson spends as much time as he can fly fishing the mountain streams of Virginia and West Virginia. He breaks down his fly choices in the following three ways.

For native brook trout and stream-born rainbows and browns, the Botetourt County, Virginia resident recommends #14-18 Elk-hair Caddis,

The North Fork of the South Branch of the Potomac River below Seneca Rocks in Pendleton County, West Virginia. Tim Kiser photo

#14-18 Parachute Adams, #14-16 Royal Wulffs, #10-14 Woolly Buggers, and #16-18 Pheasant-tail Nymphs.

For medium size water, like that which is found along the South Branch above the Smoke Hole, Alderson suggests #12-16 Elk-hair Caddis, #12-16 Parachute Adams, #10-14 LA Ants, #10-18 black Copper Johns, and #14-16 Hare's-ear Nymphs. And for bigger water, such as that found while canoeing the Smoke Hole, Kurt relies on #10 Black Nose Dace, #8-10 Beadhead Woolly Buggers, #8-10 LA Ants, #4 Chocklett Disc Popper, and the #6-8 Chocklett Gummy Minnow.

Kurt and I have already discussed a return trip to the Potomac Highlands to seek out native trout. We found this thin blue line on the *West Virginia Atlas & Gazetteer* and it looks promising. We also feel that one of the streams we explored by going upstream might turn in to quality brook trout water downstream. Chances are that you too will enjoy exploring the Potomac Watershed's trout offerings, both of the wild and stocked varieties.

4

CANOE CRUISING, PAST AND PRESENT

IN 1903, *FIELD and Stream* ran a four-part series called "Canoe Cruising on the South Branch," by B. W. Mitchell with photos by Robert Shriver. A hundred years later, I received an invitation from the Potomac River Smallmouth Club (PRSC) to go on a modern-day voyage down West Virginia's South Branch of the Potomac, retracing the same route taken by the Shawnee Canoe Club, of which Mitchell and Shriver were members.

That invitation, which resulted in a three-day float in June 2004, led me to read the four-part series so I could better understand what the South Branch and float fishing for river smallmouths was like then, and, in turn, hopefully gain a better understanding of the challenges the river and its smallmouth fishery face in the future.

Interestingly, only once in Part I did the author Mitchell, floating along in his canoe— "light dancing house of ours riding cork-like on the ripples"—mention the word *bass*. Instead, Mitchell devoted much space to the "tragic days of war," a reference to the Civil War which had ended less than 40 years previously and which was much on the minds of the trip's participants.

In Part II, Mitchell covered in depth the journey to the put-in point

Canoe cruising on the South Branch of the Potomac: 1903 style and today

via "a wheezy old locomotive, her fires gleaming through cracks in the fire box, pulling in about a half hour late after a violent fit of asthma at the foot of the grade." Much of the rest of the story pertains to the Civil War and the deeds of "good old Lewis Edmunson, noblest negro of them all, guide and scout by choice for the Union armies . . ."

Of great interest was the fact that Mitchell was concerned with what was happening to the South Branch's watershed: "now the lumberman is cursing the mountain sides with his abhorrent work." The early 20th century was the beginning of a period when timber companies pillaged the mountains of West Virginia and much of the Southeast, causing horrific erosion, the siltation and subsequent loss of many brook trout streams, and the near extinction of deer and turkeys.

Also of note is that the sporting ethic had not yet begun as Mitchell records that the Hampshire County courthouse had only issued three hunting and fishing licenses in four years. Instead of following hunting and fishing ethics, "these rascals kill mercilessly out of season and dynamite and seine the streams."

In Part III, Mitchell, finally, deals with some how-to tactics. He rates the best baits as a Paw-Paw spoon ("a deadly bait when you have learned how to cast it"), the Professor ("the killing fly for these waters"), and "a succulent shining minnow." Those baits work well for the "king of American fresh water game fishes," as Mitchell held the same high opinion for stream smallies that river runners of today have.

Mitchell also gives credit to William Shriver, a cousin of Robert's, for stocking the Potomac system with smallmouth bass in 1853. Once released, the smallmouths found "the crystal waters to their liking and the native fishes [sunfish, white perch, fall fish, suckers, and eels] an easy mark for their pugnacity and greed, they literally swarmed up and down the Potomac, and up the South Branch to its source." Today, the PRSC gives its William Shriver Award to the individual who annually catches and releases the greatest number of trophy smallmouths.

Part III also has Mitchell dealing with another environmental problem on the Potomac system, one that continued for many decades. Then "the pulp mill at Piedmont had poisoned the river [the North Branch of the

A good selection of surface flies for smallmouth.

Potomac] till it resembled frothy ink." To extract the wood for that pulp, Mitchell describes the timber concern as "destroying the entire region by denudation and defilement."

Part IV is where Mitchell gave most of the Shawnee Canoe Club's trip account from their put-in above the entrance of the Trough, downstream to the confluence with the North Branch, a distance of just over 50 miles.

RECREATING HISTORY

On June 22, 2004, PRSC members Ron Marafioti, Peter Pfotenhauer, Steve Copps, trip organizer Paul Parfomak, and I left Eagle's Nest Outfitters in Petersburg to begin our re-creation of the historic float.

Parfomak's pre-trip planning had revealed that it would be impossible for us to replicate the original excursion. For example, the Shawnee Club launched at the mouth of Mud Lick Run below the Old Fields Bridge (the bridge is where my group put-in). The mouth of Mud Lick, then and now, is on private land, but in those older, simpler times, landowners were apparently much more likely to allow people to cross their properties

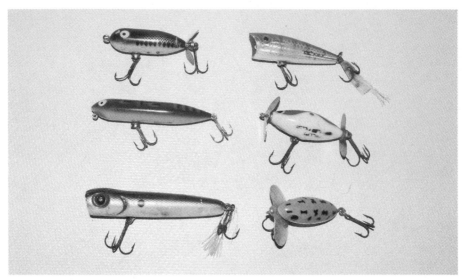

A selection of lures for smallies.

to reach the river. Of course, far fewer people were floating rivers then, which partially explains this tolerance.

After overnighting at the mouth of Mud Lick Run, Shriver and company paddled only a few miles to spend the first night at what they called "Camp Delightful," on a low water gravel bar in the Trough. Modern-day canoe campers might not understand at first why the Shawnee Club journeyed such a short distance. But the Trough, then and now, is true wilderness country and stunningly beautiful. High mountain walls, heavily forested, envelop the South Branch and massive boulders line the river. Every time I have floated through the Trough, I have viewed bald eagles, and my canoe mate Paul Parfomak and I saw three of these majestic birds. Interestingly, Shriver's group makes no mention of observing eagles, but since that time period was before the near extirpation of eagles because of DDT, I believe it likely that they not only glimpsed eagles but also saw so many that they regarded the sightings as unremarkable.

Through extensive research and the aid of a GPS unit, Parfomak felt that he had a good idea of where Camp Delightful was, so our party had our day one lunch on perhaps the same low water gravel bar where the Shawnee Canoe Club spent their night number two. Author B. W.

Gearing up for canoe camping enhances the Potomac experience.

Mitchell stated, understandably, that the club was "loth [sic] to leave all this magnificence" of the Trough, so his group spent yet another night in this area, that time camping at a massive cliff face he called Shelving Rock (Camp of Rocky Rock).

From his research, Parfomak believes that our paddling predecessors spent three days and two nights in the Trough, which extends just 7 miles, and then made a mad dash to the confluence, covering 30.25 miles on day four and 13.25 miles on day five. Parfomak and company decided to cover our version of the float in three days, paddling from Old Fields Bridge to Wapacoma Family Campground (west of Romney) on day one (18 miles), Wapacoma to Milleson's Walnut Grove Campground (near Millesons Mill) on day two (17 miles), and the campground to the Indian Rock access point (16 miles) on day three. To our frustration, we found that we could not legally take out at the confluence because it is on private land, thus the Indian Rock take-out, 4.5 miles above the union of the South and North Branches. The issue of private property rights was also why we could not duplicate the other overnight stops of the Shawnee Club. That and the fact

Canoe Camping

In addition to dry storage, fishing gear, binoculars, and guides, you'll need quality camping gear, including a mummy bag with a compression sack and a quality sleeping pad. Since I also will canoe camp in the spring and fall when the temperatures will often dip into the upper 30s to low 40s, I purchased a Eureka Silver City sleeping bag that is rated to +30. If the night is overly warm, I repose on top of the bag. For a pad, a number of years ago I bought a self-inflating sleeping pad from Campmor.

Camping enthusiast Josh Ward, who works for Blue Heron Communications, offers up this gear list for canoe campers.

Tent
Sleeping bag
Float bags or boxes
Coleman Perfect Flow InstaStart 2-Burner Stove
Cooler (size depending on number of campers) with food
Dishes, pans, kitchen utensils
Biodegradable soap
Ice or ice substitutes
Garbage sacks
Layered clothing
Wading shoes; shoes to keep dry, warm
Coleman LED Quad Lantern
Coleman 3AAA LED Headlamp
Coleman 2D or 4D Auto-On Flashlight (floats, turns on when dropped in water)
Personal flotation device
Fire starters (waterproof matches, wind/waterproof lighter)
First aid kit
Toiletries (includes paper towels and toilet paper)
2.5-Gallon expandable water carrier (enough to supply ample fresh water for all participants) [Note: author likes to also bring a water purification system.]
Towels
Extra batteries
Extra stove fuel
Compass/maps
Rain gear
Cutlery (pocket knife, camp knife, packable saw, multi-tool)
Extra rope, cord or wire for tying off canoes or re-rigging tents
Quality insect repellant
Sunscreen

that club members had a habit of making up their own place names. For example, one of their stops was called Camp Mishap (their fourth camp) because cooked eggs were dropped there.

The Shawnee members were gentleman anglers, wearing bow ties and suspenders while they fished and camped. They also sometimes left the river, once stopping at a Wapacoma hotel (their last lunch on the float). So on our day two with the intention of exploring the community, I debarked from my canoe at the Route 50 bridge in Romney to throw out some of our trash, visit the local library and check my e-mail, and mail off several rolls of Kodachrome 64 (the film era was not yet over).

After we reached the Indian Rock take-out on day three of our modern-day voyage down the South Branch, we sat and talked about our re-creation of the Shawnee Club's journey as we awaited our shuttle. The most interesting question posed was whether a writer a century from now would re-create our float for his readers?

THE POTOMAC RIVER SMALLMOUTH CLUB—ANGLING CONSERVATIONISTS

One of the angling clubs that I admire the most is the Potomac River Smallmouth Club. The PRSC is a non-partisan association of conservation-minded fishermen dedicated to preserving the fisheries and water-quality in the entire Chesapeake Bay Watershed. They serve as watchdogs and as an extra set of eyes for the Maryland, Virginia, and West Virginia state fisheries managers and the Potomac Riverkeeper organization. The PRSC welcomes all interested anglers to join them at their meetings.

ON-GOING ISSUES

- Supporting Catch, Photograph, and Release of all fish caught in the Chesapeake watershed and particularly the Potomac and Shenandoah rivers.

- Promoting and supporting the efforts of all area Riverkeeper organizations.

- Supporting full access to all navigable waterways as defined under current state and federal laws and removal of archaic and unreasonable legal hindrances to the full use and enjoyment of our navigable waterways by all citizens.

- Supporting regulations that will reduce the nutrient levels in all Chesapeake Bay Watershed streams and rivers.

- Supporting improved agricultural methods that will support healthy, unpolluted, and undisturbed riparian areas along the banks of the streams and rivers of the Chesapeake Bay Watershed.

- Supporting the Conservation Easement movement in the Chesapeake Bay Watershed.

ON-GOING ACTIVITIES

- Assisting the Maryland DNR Department of Fisheries Management with creel surveys.

- Providing input for public access improvements on the Shenandoah River.

- Working with other Virginia fishing clubs to provide monofilament fishing line recycling stations for public access ramps on the Shenandoah River.

- Supporting cleanup efforts along the upper Potomac River and Shenandoah rivers.

- Providing volunteers for fundraising efforts for the Potomac and Shenandoah Riverkeepers.

Herschel Finch, conservation chairman for the PRSC, offers praise for the Riverkeeper programs in effect in the watershed, including tracking poultry litter and its use in the Shenandoah Valley, and getting many municipalities (as well as several large industrial plants and construction

---

Who First Stocked Smallmouths in the Potomac System?

Who first stocked smallmouths in the Potomac System? Arvella Zimmerer of Eagle's Nest Outfitters says that in her area a James McCuskey, an engineer on the B&O Railroad, is reputed to have first stocked smallies via railroad in the South Branch in the early 1850s.

However, as noted earlier, the Potomac River Smallmouth Club maintains that William Shriver conducted the original release, also by railroad, in the early 1850s. Whoever was first, and perhaps there were a number of other stockings as well, the West Virginia Division of Natural Resources states that smallmouth bass did not exist in the Potomac drainage before 1854.

---

sites) in the watershed to upgrade their systems to reduce their nitrogen, phosphorus, and other pollutants.

"I shudder to think where we would be without the efforts of the Potomac and Shenandoah Riverkeepers and their crack staff, especially after the fish kills we had in the early years of the new century," he said. "Brent Walls on the Potomac and Jeff Kelble on the Shenandoah along with Alan Lehman and all the staff and interns do a phenomenal job of keeping up with permits, discharges, agricultural activities and the whole host of issues affecting the water quality of the Potomac and Shenandoah. We've still got a long way to go, but we believe the Potomac and Shenandoah rivers are in good hands."

5

REPORT FROM THE UPPER POTOMAC RIVER MANAGER

Brent Walls is the Upper Potomac River Manager for the Potomac Riverkeeper (www.potomacriverkeeper.org), which basically means he is the environmental watchdog so that those of us who recreate on the upper reaches of the stream can continue to enjoy it. As noted in Chapter One, the beginning of the South Branch of the Potomac is a barn in Highland County, Virginia. The start of the North Branch is the Fairfax Stone near Kempton, Maryland.

"The headwaters of a river start at the point where groundwater breaches the surface," Walls said. "Some call these springs, but springs are found throughout a river's path, not just at the headwaters. So where does a stream start? In the study of rivers, hydrogeology, streams and rivers are categorized into "orders", that is, first order, second order and so on, and these orders identify the start and growth of a river system.

"A first order stream is the start of the waterway, that point where groundwater breaches the surface or rain collects and runs to a central low point on the landscape, the start of a watershed. Every river, stream, and creek has a watershed. Like a river, so too does a watershed grow until it reaches the ocean. In the case of the Potomac, the Chesapeake

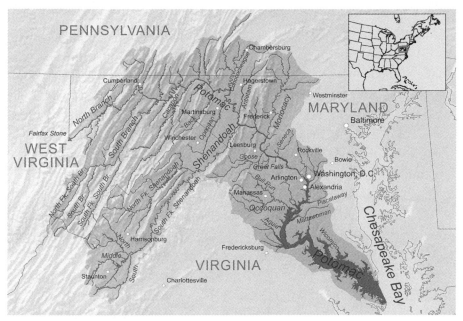

Potomac River watershed.

Bay is the end point. However, the beginning of the Potomac is not just from one point, but thousands of miles of springs and creeks."

Polluted by decades of acidic water draining out of old coal and mineral mine shafts, known as Acid Mine Drainage or AMD, the North Branch was once considered a dead stream. Walls says that in the 1800s and 1900s, when a coal mine was tunneled out of a mountainside, it was done so at an upward angle to allow for natural drainage of the mine shaft. The mine shafts exposed layers of pyrite and other minerals that when exposed to water and air, created acidic water.

When this acidic water, which contained dissolved metals, mixed with the tributaries of the North Branch, an orange slick would appear. The neutral pH of the streams allowed for the metals to slowly settle out onto the watershed's rocks. The acidic water and metal deposits would build up over time, turning the North Branch into a lifeless river. Locals in the area remember a time that the river was ignored, treated as if it were not there continues Walls.

Thanks to passage of the Surface Mining Control and Reclamation Act (SMCRA) in the 1970s, a system was put into place to regulate active mines and the older abandoned mines. SMCRA set up a fund that is financed through a tax on active mines. The funds are distributed to the states to be used on a priority projects.

Shortly thereafter, says the Riverkeeper, the Army Corp of Engineers completed construction of the Jennings Randolph Dam in 1981, which started the impressive recovery of the North Branch Potomac. For the North Branch, much of the SMCRA funds were put toward active treatment on the higher priority mine drainages. Active treatment uses calibrated lime dosers to adjust the pH as close to the mine site as possible. This treatment quickly adjusts the pH to normal; which allows the toxic metals to settle out faster and in a shorter distance.

"This gives the rest of the stream a chance to rebuild and develop a productive stream habitat," Walls said. "Nine dosers have been constructed in Maryland and three in West Virginia. By the 1990s, the North Branch started to reclaim itself as a productive and useful river. The dosers may have breathed new life in the North Branch, but without the Jennings Randolph Dam, one of the most popular cold-water fisheries in the East would never have been achieved."

The deep Jennings Randolph Lake has stratified layers of cold water, which the dam operator can extract and discharge to the North Branch. The purpose of the dam was primarily for flood control; many of the towns downstream would annually flood. The secondary purpose was for water quality, to be a buffer from upstream AMD runoff that had not been addressed yet. The bonus prize was cold water conditions in the North Branch that could support stocked brown and rainbow trout. Since the North Branch is so close to the Washington D.C. Metro area, it has become a popular destination for fishermen.

"The explosion of recreational opportunities from fishing to white-water kayaking has boosted the once starved economy with a $3 million recreational tourism industry; which has resulted in several fishing guide services, boating and recreational tours, increased wages/jobs, and infrastructure investments," said Walls. "The many successful years of productive stream habitat growth has created conditions for the successful spawning of trout. These wild trout are noticeably more vibrant in color and more ferocious on the line than stocked fish. The recovery of the North Branch Potomac has been a remarkable achievement."

However, the vibrantly productive North Branch Potomac may not have a bright future. Walls says that each one of the dosers that continuously preserves the proper pH of the mine drainage has to be maintained. These maintenance costs are taken out of the allotted funds from SMRCA; however, these funds will stop in 2025 and the availability of the money for maintaining dosers may end as early as 2017. If Congress or Maryland do not develop a contingency plan to maintain the progress that has been achieved thus far, the North Branch will see a return to more polluted waters fears Walls. Other issues have also arisen.

"Every dam that is built has a life expectancy and the Jennings Randolph Dam has less life than originally predicted," Walls said. "The steep slopes, active surface mining, and intense rain events have increased sediment run off to the lake, filling the depths and decreasing the water capacity. The cold-water fishery of the North Branch depends on the deep cold water of the lake and once the lake starts to fill in, it will be difficult to maintain cold-water discharges.

"The priorities of the lake seem to have shifted from water quality of the North Branch to maintaining beachfront access on the lake during the summer. And with a newly proposed hydroelectric addition to the dam, the priorities of the lake are gravitating away from a healthy North Branch fishery. The retention of water during the summer for beach use and the diversion of water for power lessens the amount of water released to achieve cold temperatures down the entire length of the North Branch.

"Temperatures in the downstream sections are reaching into the 90s, virtually boiling the fish. The stressed conditions have resulted in fish kills and threaten the naturally reproducing trout. The protection of the cold-water fisheries is vital for the river and the economy of the area."

In addition to the North Branch's issues, upper Potomac enthusiasts will have to keep close watch on other potential threats.

"The Potomac has a range of pollution issues from urbanized storm

Earlier in this century, skin lesions in game fish were all too common on the Potomac watershed.

through the state and have weak protections. Others like farms are exempt from permits and regulations but have devastating cumulative effects. Since all water builds as it flows downstream, so too does pollution.

"The Potomac headwaters, the thousands of first-order streams, are primarily in rural areas where farming or mining activities take place. These stream sections are plagued by nutrients, herbicides, and AMD. As the streams flow downstream, growing in size as streams merge, they reach more populated areas where storm water, waste treatment facilities, and industry start to foul the water. As any river become more polluted downstream, the threat to people increases. But the headwaters are where things start and where the most work always needs to be done."

Walls relates that it is difficult for many to know if a stream is polluted, unless there is a visible mess or an extremely obnoxious odor. One of the biggest concerns is the health of the fish and since we eat the fish, our health can become a concern, too. Each state now has fish consumption advisories after major pollution spills and recommendations for healthy proportions of fish to eat based on mercury levels from our country's burning of coal.

All of these are invisible problems. But in the first years of this century, visible problems began to also occur in the Potomac Watershed. Many fish were found to possess skin lesions and abscesses. About the same time these reports were coming in from the headwaters of the South Branch of the Potomac and other tributaries, massive fish kills occurred. Then another issue arose—intersex fish.

"Several fish species in the South Branch of the Potomac, Shenandoah, Main Stem of the Potomac, and now in several other parts of the country have both male and female sex organs," Walls said. "First found in small-mouth bass by the U.S.G.S. on the South Branch, this curious genetic mutation exploded into a frenzy of questions. Now, spearheaded by U.S.G.S. Fisheries Biologist Vicky Blazer, the hunt for what caused this mutation is in full swing.

"Since intersex fish have been found in both populated and rural areas, the question still remains what is the cause. Correlations between agricultural areas and intensity of intersex fish are increasingly more significant, but an exact cause is still undetermined. So now, along with fish consumption advisories from spills and mercury deposits, we have fish with invisible mutations, unknown causes, and unknown health effects to us. Not only do we eat the fish, but we drink the water that the fish live in and our water treatment facilities are not designed to remove the possible chemicals that are the culprit."

Despite these issues, I have faith that through the efforts of the Potomac Riverkeeper and conservation groups like the Potomac River Smallmouth Club and others, the Potomac Watershed will continue to be what it has always been—one of America's great and most important ecosystems.

PART II

THE SOUTH BRANCH
OF THE POTOMAC
(WEST VIRGINIA)

6

BIG BEND TO VERNON WELTON PARK

U.S.G.S QUADS:
Upper Tract and Petersburg West

DISTANCE:
23 miles

RAPIDS:
Class Is, IIs, and IIIs; Chimney Slide is a Class III-IV

ACCESS POINTS:
At Big Bend (Pendleton County), there is a gravel/dirt ramp on river left off Smoke Hole Road. Parking is limited. Vernon Welton Park (Grant County) on Route 220 north in Petersburg has two concrete ramps on river left with abundant parking. Paddlers who go with Eagle's Nest Outfitters can take out at the company's access point at their base store on river left off Route 220 in Petersburg, less than a mile upstream from Vernon Welton Park.

IT WAS A moment in my sporting life that I will always remember. As the sun slowly went down, Doak Harbison, Tim Wimer, and I sat around a campfire with Steve Copps and his daughter, Cammie, and son-in-law, Ross Fuller. Heating up wild turkey leg soup (the main ingredient of which came from a Marshall County bird I had killed the previous fall), I thought about how beautiful and perfect the venue and the sun's setting both were. Amazingly, the time was not even 6:00 p.m, but because of the towering mountains enveloping us, deep shadows stretched across the river and

Paddling the Smoke Hole is a true wilderness experience. Mountains tower above the river on both its sides throughout the Smoke Hole, the 1,000-feet deep canyon adding to the splendid isolation.

our campsite on the famed Smoke Hole section of the South Branch of the Potomac. My quintet was on a three-day excursion down what has to be one of the most stunningly gorgeous sections of any Eastern river.

Arvella Zimmerer, who along with her husband John, operates Eagle's Nest Outfitters in Petersburg. She feels that the upper reaches of the South Branch offer the best smallmouth action.

"The Upper South Branch has always had better bass fishing than the lower part," says Arvella. "The Smoke Hole section itself is one of the few places in West Virginia where float fishermen can catch trout and small-mouths. And when bald eagles were scarce just about everywhere else, we saw them in the canyon.

"The best smallmouth fishing in the upper half of the river is below the Smoke Hole in the first catch-and-release area, which starts at the Petersburg

Gap Bridge. I would say that the best time to visit the upper river is during the spring and summer depending on, of course, water levels and clarity."

And bird watchers and nature lovers will likely be enthralled as well.

"There's been a new addition to the Smoke Hole," said Arvella Zimmerer in response to my question if any change had taken place in this wilderness section that envelops the upper South Branch of the Potomac. Her response surprised me, as change rarely comes to this isolated region of West Virginia's Potomac Highlands.

After all, the first big change could be considered the arrival of the Native Americans who used the caves that dot the steep mountainsides to live in and cook their meat. The smoke from those many fires gave the region its name. Later, pioneers homesteaded the valley and eked out a meager living with their cattle and crops. The next major change was when Mountain State moonshiners discovered those same caves and utilized them to practice their particular kind of brewing. Arvella's change was a welcome one.

"Around 2003, golden eagles began appearing in the Smoke Hole, and, now, apparently, they're breeding here," continued Arvella.

For years, I had been yearning to return to the Smoke Hole and make the 23-mile float from Big Bend to Arvella and John Zimmerer's base livery at Eagle's Nest Outfitters in Petersburg. On my other visits, my wife, Elaine, and I had been enthralled by the splendid isolation, bald eagles, challenging rapids, and fishing for smallmouth bass and trout.

Less than a mile into our excursion, my canoe mate Doak Harbison shouted out "Golden eagle at 11:00 o'clock," causing me to put down my paddle and scan the sky.

Sure enough, the large wingspan (some 7 feet), huge head and neck, and white tail base were unmistakable identification marks. A few minutes later, a second golden eagle joined the first one and together they rode the air currents above the river—giving credence to Arvella Zimmerer's contention that these raptors are common in the Smoke Hole.

The South Branch has more bald and golden eagles than any other river I have paddled. How do you tell them apart? Adult bald eagles feature a white head and tail, and the golden a golden-brown nape. Young

The upper South Branch as it flows above and through the Smoke Hole offers trout as well as smallmouth action.

bald eagles lack the white head and tail and look much more like adult golden eagles. To distinguish a young bald, look for its pale wing linings.

Conversely, immature golden eagles have a great deal of white in their tails, leading them sometimes to be mistaken for a young bald. Note, however, that the tails of juvenile goldens are white at the base and black at the tip—a major distinguishing feature. They also flaunt white patches on the undersides of their wings. As is true with almost all birds, the two eagles make distinctive calls, and, if all else fails, the voices of these two raptors can serve to distinguish them. Bald eagles utter a cackling sound (kak-kak-kak) while goldens are largely silent except for occasional whistles.

The Smoke Hole is indeed a birder's paradise. During that excursion, I tallied 39 species just from our canoe. We saw eight golden eagles, two bald eagles, as well as Baltimore orioles, Louisiana waterthrush, scarlet tanagers, yellow warblers, and ravens. I have no doubt that I could have added several dozen more species if I had ventured into the surrounding mountains and fields of the Monongahela National Forest, which surrounds the river in most places with only a few smatterings of private land. Those same fields are also the homes of vestige populations of prairie plants. Amazingly, prickly pear cacti, Indian grass, and little bluestem thrive in the Smoke Hole—just as they did thousands of years ago.

Paddling the Smoke Hole is a true wilderness experience, as the only dwelling in the Smoke Hole proper is the now-closed Smoke Hole Lodge, once owned by Eddie Stifel III. Mountains tower above the river on both its sides throughout the Smoke Hole, the 1,000-feet deep canyon adding to the splendid isolation.

That said, Arvella Zimmerer cautions that the Smoke Hole hosts some major rapids, which can be dangerous to negotiate, especially during the high water of spring. Guided trips are certainly an option.

For the earlier mentioned float, I paired with Doak Harbison in a canoe, which was also the Fullers' mode of transportation, while Steve Copps and Tim Wimer opted to fish from kayaks. Since I was the only one who had paddled the Smoke Hole, Harbison and I led the way.

On the first mile of the float, you'll see the aptly named Eagle Rock on river right, as well as drift through some Class I ledges. For the second mile, the river forms a river left outside bend with a rock garden and with numerous riffles and places to fish.

A Class I appears near the end of the second mile, and then the pace of this daughter of the Potomac accelerates. You will next come to a Class I-II, which should be run on river right. Some downstream eddies conceal smallies and trout, and you'll float by some fields on river left and cliffs on the opposite side.

After flowing relatively straight for about a mile, the river forms a sharp river right bend, which, in turn, leads to a more gradual river left bend. Not long past mile 4, you will come to Shook Gap and Smoke Hole Lodge. The Nature Conservancy has purchased a conservation easement on the 1,126-acre tract of the closed lodge. This easement will prevent development, logging, and mining along nearly three miles of the South Branch.

Next, you will pass through a Class II, which can be portaged on river right, and a slab rock. As you pass mile 6, be prepared for some rough water. My wife, Elaine, and I once overturned when we slammed into a mid-river boulder that Arvella Zimmerer has dubbed Eddie's Rock. But the major danger is the Class III-IV Chimney Slide. This is an extremely dangerous rapid that I have portaged on river right every time I have come to it. Two large boulders guard the sides of this rapid, which the Zimmerers have dubbed King and Queen. A boulder named The Joker guards the middle passage and heralds a 10-foot drop.

Thankfully, the river now slows its pace. Between the 7- and 8-mile point, the massive and spectacular Blue Rock appears. A creek dribbling in on river right also marks this area, which has a Class I. Some people also like to camp on river right through here.

Between miles 9 and 10, Redman Gap looms on river left and Redman Run also enters on that same side. The river now flows in long, deep pools and Austin Run and Austin Gap come up on river left between miles 10 and 11. For the next several miles, action for smallies and trout can be good in the numerous riffles.

At about mile 14, the North Fork of the South Branch enters on river left. Eddies and a river left cliff also characterize this area. You have now left the Smoke Hole proper.

Over the next mile-plus, you will pass under a power line and through a long pool and some riffles. Then the treacherous remains of the Royal Glen Dam loom, a solid Class III rapid with a 10-foot hole. Concrete rebars stud the bottom at the dam site, creating a hazard for human and boat alike. I strongly recommend that you not run this rapid. You can drag a craft over boulders and dam remnants on river right or ask to gain permission to portage on private land on river left.

After you portage the dam site, you will see some cliffs on river right. At about mile 17 you encounter the Class I-II Smith Falls, which should be run on river right. Then come two Class I-II rapids, Big Daddy and Big Mama, which are followed by three Class I ledges. Just past mile 20, you pass under the Route 220 Petersburg Bridge and come to a series of islands and Lunice Creek on river left. I have caught some nice smallies in this area. Below that confluence, you will pass by some boulders and a Class I and eventually come to the Eagle's Nest Outfitters take-out on river left in the Petersburg Gap area. Not far downstream lies Vernon Welton Park.

7

VERNON WELTON PARK TO FISHER BRIDGE SOUTH

U.S.G.S QUADS:
Petersburg West, Maysville, Petersburg East, and Rig

DISTANCE:
5.5 miles

RAPIDS:
Class Is and a Class II

ACCESS POINTS:
Two concrete ramps on river left at Vernon Welton Park (Grant County) on Route 220 north in Petersburg. Parking spaces are abundant. At Fisher Bridge South (Hardy County), the take-out is a concrete ramp on river right off Route 220. Parking is limited.

NOT LONG AFTER you launch at Vernon Welton Park, you pass under the Petersburg Gap Bridge (Routes 28, 55, and 220). From here downstream 8 miles to the Route 13 Fisher Bridge, all black bass caught must be returned to the water at once. This section is known as the Area 1 Catch-and-Release section. Despite the catch-and-release designation, the first mile of this float offers unremarkable habitat, as you will drift through a deep pool, riffle, and a shallow section. I suggest that you quickly paddle through this area.

Now begins what for me has been some of the consistently best fishing on the South Branch of the Potomac. Over the quarter century or so that

The view at the Petersburg Gap.

I have fished this river, I would guess that I have floated this trip and the next one the most. I don't recall ever doing poorly on these two floats, and some of the outings have been outstanding.

In the summer, the topwater action can be especially explosive. Fly fishers should have plenty of poppers and damsel and dragonfly patterns, and spinning enthusiasts should bring along Heddon Tiny Torpedoes and Zara Spooks, Phillips Crippled Killers, Rebel Pop-R's, and the best floating-diving minnow bait ever—the Rapala Original Minnow.

Just before mile 2, the river bends to the left and a rock cliff towers above. An island then dots the river and sunken ledges and boulders offer angling opportunities over the next mile. Next is what the Zimmerers of Eagle's Nest Outfitters label as the O-Hell rapid, a Class II at a sharp river right bend. The couple suggests that you keep to the left side of this rapid or portage on river left. Boulders line the river right side and more large rocks stud the middle section. Downstream looms another scenic cliff and more ledges and riffles to Class Is. A string of cabins also lie on the left shoreline. An island also cleaves the river, too. The smallmouth action picks up considerably through this area.

The river then straightens for several miles and a railroad track parallels much of the river right shoreline. A golf course also lies along this bank. Numerous boulders and trees (especially overhanging sycamores) line river right. This entire section offers outstanding smallmouth sport, and over the years I have caught and released numerous quality bass here. Soon you will come to the Fisher Bridge South access point on river right.

8

FISHER BRIDGE SOUTH
TO FISHER BRIDGE

U.S.G.S QUADS:
Petersburg East and Rig

DISTANCE:
2.5 miles

RAPIDS:
Class Is and IIs

ACCESS POINTS:
At Fisher Bridge South (Hardy County), the put-in is a concrete ramp on river right off Route 220. Parking is limited. At Fisher Bridge (Hardy County), the take-out is a concrete ramp on river right at the Route 13 Fisher Bridge, which can be reached via Route 220. Parking is available.

THE CATCH-AND-RELEASE SECTION continues on and extends throughout the Fisher Bridge South float, and the fishing for bass remains good. A rocky river left bank, a braided channel, and numerous riffles characterize the first mile of this float—which makes for a fine evening after-work getaway. In the next section, which comes after a short river left bend, some trees have been known to fall into the river, and they can make for some serious obstructions. Portaging may be required. Often the best channel is the middle one.

The river then immediately curves to the right and you will see a river right island, which seems to be on the verge of silting in on its right side.

The Fisher Bridge float features a lot of vegetation to draw fish.

The river then straightens and passes by some fields on river left. Riffles and Class I to II rapids and ledges characterize the last mile of the float. Riprap also lies on the river right shoreline and you will spot a huge rock on the left shoreline known as Zim's Rock. You will want to probe this entire area carefully with your lures or flies. Fisher Bridge signals the end of the first catch-and-release section.

9

FISHER BRIDGE TO OLD FIELDS BRIDGE

U.S.G.S QUADS:
Petersburg East and Rig
DISTANCE:
4.5 miles
RAPIDS:
Riffles
ACCESS POINTS:
At Fisher Bridge (Hardy County), the put-in is a concrete ramp on river right at the Route 13 Fisher Bridge, which can be reached via Route 220. Parking is available. At Old Fields Bridge (Hardy County), a rock/dirt ramp is on river right off a dirt lane via County Route 15 (Cunningham Lane) and Route 220/28. Parking is limited.

S OME RIFFLES SANDWICH a slow moving pool at the start of this float, and this type of water characterizes the entire Fisher Bridge float. The fishing on this float is often better in the spring and fall than in the summer. If the river is low and the water hot during the dog days, for example, fishing can be challenging on this section.

For the first mile, the river flows straight until a gentle river left curve occurs and more riffles appear. Anglers should focus their efforts in these and other riffles, as no Class I or II rapids exist to concentrate the

A nice smallmouth caught near Fisher Bridge.

bronzebacks. The river then resumes flowing in a fairly straight fashion for another mile or so until it makes a gentle river right curve.

The community of Moorefield lies beyond river right, and it is also here that the South Fork of the South Branch enters on river right. Once again, the river straightens and flows placidly. Indeed, that is the river's pace for the rest of this float, except for the occasional riffle. The major feature in this section is Goat Hill, a massive bare spot on river left that can be easily seen from well upriver as well as from Routes 220/28. The Old Fields Bridge marks the end of this float. Though I do not recommend fishing fans take this trip during the summer, parents who like to take their offspring on gentle junkets will find this excursion much to their liking and can enjoy a leisurely two- to three-hour getaway.

10

OLD FIELDS BRIDGE to TROUGH ENTRANCE (SOUTH BRANCH WMA)

U.S.G.S QUADS:
Moorefield and Old Fields
DISTANCE:
5 miles
RAPIDS:
Class Is and riffles.
ACCESS POINTS:
At Old Fields Bridge (Hardy County), a rock/dirt ramp is on river right off a dirt lane via County Route 15 (Cunningham Lane) and Route 220/28. Parking is limited. At the Trough Entrance (Hardy County), access is via County Route 6 on river right. Parking is limited.

THE OLD FIELDS float is the first on the lower South Branch, and it is also one of my favorites on the lower section. This is a good trip to encounter plenty of 12- to 14-inch smallmouths (depending on recent spawning success of course) as well as occasional bigger fish.

The first mile of this trip contains a number of rocky banks, especially on river right, as well as numerous riffles. This is a fine section to toss top-water lures and flies, and I have had a good deal of success doing so. At mile 1, an island cleaves the river—take the right route for the most water.

Less than a half mile of paddling later, you will come to two large islands; paddle down the middle of them. After doing so, you will spot another

The Old Fields Bridge float is just one of many quality ones on the South Branch.

island, this one on river right; scoot down its left side. At about mile 2, the South Branch forms a gentle river right bend. On the South Branch, the outside bends typically offer good smallmouth action, as woody debris often accumulates. If those bends have sycamores and other water-loving trees such as silver maples, speckled alders, and river birches, all the better. Of all those tree species, sycamores are most likely to produce the best bass action, as the root wads of sycamores offers excellent cover. But don't pass up any kind of wood cover or shade.

After you leave the outside bend, the next major feature is a Class I rapid; the best pathway is on river right. The South Branch then flows straight for well over a mile before another river right bend forms just before mile 4; several small islands are in this vicinity. Stony Run then enters on river right, followed by a Class I and riffle, which mark your approach to the Trough.

11

TROUGH ENTRANCE (SOUTH BRANCH WMA) TO HARMISONS

U.S.G.S. QUADS:
Old Fields and Sector

DISTANCE:
7 miles

RAPIDS:
Riffles, Class Is, and a Class II

ACCESS POINTS:
At the Trough entrance (Hardy County), access is via County Route 6 on river right. Parking is limited. At Harmisons (Hampshire County), there is a long concrete ramp on river right off County Route 8 via Route 50. Parking is available.

A RVELLA ZIMMERER AND her husband, John, operate Eagle's Nest Outfitters in Petersburg; she proclaims that river fans come from all over the country come to float the famous Trough, which has been attracting smallmouth enthusiasts for over a century. Zimmerer also rates this float, the Old Fields one, and the Romney Bridge trip as among the best on the lower river.

The Trough, so named because of the high mountain walls that envelope much of this float, is one of the most unusual places I have ever fished. Because of those mountains, a stiff wind blows much if not most of the time when you are floating through here. And much of that time,

The enveloping mountains are part of the appeal of The Trough.

the wind seems to be blowing upstream, making paddling an exhausting affair. The Trough is also scenic as the wooded mountainsides give a wild flavor to the float.

Despite Arvella raving about the fishing potential for the Trough trip, I have more often than not struggled here. It seems that I never visit this section at the right time, as either a cold front or high, muddy water seem to follow me whenever I come here. I guess I am just out of sync with this section of river.

This and the Smoke Hole are my favorite places to raptor watch on the South Branch. Expect an opportunity to glimpse both bald and golden eagles, as well as red-tailed and broad-winged hawks among the buteo clan. And among the accipiter contingent, look for sharp-shins and Cooper hawks. Keep your binoculars handy so that you can exult in glassing these magnificent raptors.

A challenging Class II occurs at the beginning of the trek; run this rapid on river right. Below a bridge comes a Class I, which should be run on river left. Outstanding smallmouth fishing can exist in the push water above the South Branch's rapids and the eddies and runs below. Linger in this type of area. A number of boulders also dot the river throughout the Trough, and this cover likewise holds smallmouths.

Numerous riffles and boulders characterize the second mile of the Trough, and the splendid isolation continues, as the only sign of man is the railroad track that parallels the river left bank. Indeed, this type of scenery and cover continues throughout the next several miles. The only thing that could spoil your float and reverie is, again, the stiff wind that always seems to be blowing upstream.

At about mile 5, a Class I-II rapid rears up. A white house near the hamlet of Wickham warns that the rapid is near. A great profusion of rocky cover lies below this rapid. Past mile 6, Sawmill Run enters on river right. The Harmisons take-out lies below.

12

HARMISONS TO ROMNEY BRIDGE

U.S.G.S QUADS:
Sector and Romney

DISTANCE:
10.25 miles

RAPIDS:
Riffles, Class Is, and a Class II

ACCESS POINTS:
At Harmisons (Hampshire County), there is a long concrete ramp on river right off County Route 8 via Route 50. Parking is available. At the Route 50 Romney Bridge (Hampshire County), there is a rock/dirt access point on river left. Parking is available at the bridge. A dirt road leads from Route 50 down to the river.

AFTER FLOATING THROUGH the "air tunnel" that is the Trough, float fishermen will see their horizons noticeably broaden after they pass the Harmisons access point. A number of riffles characterize the first mile and the river left shoreline remains wooded. Fish around the many rocks. Fields predominate on river right; River Road runs along that shoreline as well.

Just before mile 3, Stony Run enters on river right. This is upstream from the community of Pancake on river left—just another of the many colorful place names in the Mountain State. At about mile 4, an island that has a red barn and white silo nearby is on river left. The waterway

The Harmisons float offers fine smallmouth sport.

next takes a river right bend, and, in order, you come an island, which should be run on its right, a Class I ledge, and numerous rocky pools and shoreline eddies. Also in this bend, Buffalo Run enters on river right above the island, and this area provides outstanding fishing.

The South Branch then takes a delicate turn to the left (numerous rocks exist in this bend) before straightening at mile 6. Now it is the river right shoreline's turn to be heavily wooded. The stream next forms a dogleg to the right and then transforms into a river left bend where the mountainside is heavily wooded. Camp Wapacoma lies on river right and makes a convenient place to camp for the night.

It was also on this float that I once experienced a casting mishap and a hook from one of my lures became embedded in my canoe mate, Paul Parfomak. I felt terrible because Paul's pain was entirely my fault. Over the years, I have twice had lure hooks enter my body, once in my forehead and the other time in a finger, and both times I was in real agony. Fortunately, we had a first aid kit and fellow paddlers Ron Marafioti, Peter Pfotenhauer, and Steve Copps knew how to remove a hook by using the "line tension" gambit. The easiest way to remove an embedded hook, specifically if the hook barb has come all the way through the skin, is to simply cut off the hook and barb and then back out the rest of the hook through the wound channel. That's why I always carry pliers that will cut through a hook.

Plenty of good cover lines the shores below Camp Wapacoma, and riffles are common. Afterwards, though, the river deepens and slows, as does the bass action. Mill Run enters on river right. Riffles, a Class II, and underwater rocky cover are worth checking over the course of the next mile or so, and I once saw two bald eagles at the same time in this stretch. As you near Romney, summer homes and camps will appear more and more, especially on river right. An island lies upstream from the Romney Bridge, as do eddies and lots of rocky cover—all of which receive heavy fishing pressure because of the proximity to this town. This is a grand float and another of my favorites.

13

ROMNEY BRIDGE TO BLUE BEACH BRIDGE

U.S.G.S. QUADS:
Romney, Augusta, Headsville, and Springfield
DISTANCE:
9.5 miles
RAPIDS:
A Class II at the Romney Bridge, Class Is, and riffles
ACCESS POINTS:
At the Route 50 Romney Bridge (Hampshire County), there is a rock/dirt access point on river left. Parking is available at the bridge. A dirt road leads from Route 50 down to the river. At the Route 28 Blue Beach Bridge (Hampshire County), turn onto County Route 28-5. The road runs along river left; access is via wide spots in the road. Parking is limited.

ROMNEY BRIDGE BEGINS a 9.5-mile-long section of catch-and-release black bass water that continues until Blue Beach Bridge. On previous excursions, I have caught smallmouths up to 18 inches on this float. This is known as Area 2 or the second catch-and-release section. A tricky Class II rapid swirls around the Romney Bridge; consider portaging around it on either side if you have doubts about running it.

The first mile of this float features fields, water willows, riffles, and pools. A mountain lies beyond the B&O Railroad tracks on river left and Romney resides on the opposite side. You will also pass by a large island,

The Romney Bridge float features lots of quality smallie sport.

which should be run on its left. Below the island lies some excellent habitat in the form of riffles and more water willow beds. After mile 1, a railroad bridge crosses the waterway and before mile 2 you will spot the remains of a wing dam. Plenty of riffles flow between several pools. Next, Big Run enters on river right, and the river slows a great deal for several miles.

Although the fishing is only fair during these few miles, the bird watching can be good. One bird in particular I want to mention—the Eastern kingbird. When I first started visiting the South Branch in the late 1980s, I never saw one. But when the new century started, kingbirds began making their way back to the river, especially areas where they could perch on an old snag overlooking a field.

Kingbirds, which have a diagnostic white tip on their tail and a white throat, chest, and belly, are members of the flycatcher family and are outstanding predators of all manners of flying bugs. I am seeing them more and more places now, including my own backyard. Other "good" birds along the river to look for are orchard orioles, common yellowthroats, and yellow-throated vireos just to name a few. In the summertime, a grove of sycamores almost always possesses an orchard oriole or two.

At about the 4½-mile point, the quality habitat returns as you pass by two small islands and the river takes a quick, short turn and forms a river left bend and a large eddy. A series of eddies will bring you away from there and soon you will spot the magnificent Hanging Rock on river right. This stunning cliff has been a marker for generations of South Branch voyagers. If you enjoy taking scenic shots, this is a must stop. If you enjoy catching nice smallmouths, upstream and down from this area offers potential.

About a half mile later, Fox Run enters on river left and the pace of the South Branch slows for a while. At mile 6, the river creates a long, gentle river left bend. Fields lie on the river left side during the first part of the curve. Coming out of the bend, you will enter some slow water, which is followed by more riffles and another series of deep pools. These pools are classic late winter and early spring smallmouth habitat, but the action can be slow in warmer weather. In this general area, you will see a steep bluff on river left and an eroded hillside. Summer homes on river right will let you know you are nearing Blues Beach.

14

BLUE BEACH BRIDGE TO MILLESONS MILL

U.S.G.S QUAD:
  Springfield
DISTANCE:
  9.5 miles
RAPIDS:
  Class Is and riffles
ACCESS POINTS:
  At the Route 28 Blue Beach Bridge (Hampshire County), turn onto County Route 28-5. The road runs along river left; access is via wide spots in the road. Parking is extremely limited. At Millesons Mill (Hampshire County), access is at the County Route 3 Bridge on river right (via Route 28). There is a concrete ramp; parking is available.

A T THE BEGINNING of this trip, quality shoreline cover attracts wade and bank fishermen. Water willow beds and summer homes on river right also characterize this section. At mile 1, you will come to an island, and the next mile is marked by riffles and small islands. A long river right curve then forms and within you will encounter riffles, grass beds, and a rolling Class I. Millesons Campground lies on the river left bank and is yet another place where overnight camping is available. Some beautiful cliffs also dot the river on river right.

Water willow beds are the true staff of life on our waterways. This

The Blue Beach Bridge float, as is true of much of the South Branch, offers great smallmouth action.

float, like all of the ones on the South Branch, hosts numerous water willow beds. And in any season, anglers should be aware of their presence. In the winter, barren water willow beds that border deep-water pools or drop-offs draw smallies. Toss a jig and pig or a tube bait into the drop-off and retrieve it slowly.

In the spring, the emergent vegetation will entice smallies looking to move shallow for the spawn. Slow roll a spinnerbait or work a crankbait through the area; fly fishermen should opt for a Clouser Minnow or any kind of streamer. Come summer, smallies will patrol water willow beds in search of damsel and dragonflies. Long rodders can take advantage of this with any kind of popper; spin fishermen can do the same with a prop bait or a buzzbait. And in the fall as the vegetation slowly dies, the same tactics that worked in the spring will once again catch fish.

The South Branch then straightens but soon forms a river-left bend. A Class I-II rapid lies within and should be run left of center. At about mile 5, you will course through another series of riffles; and fields will dot the river right shore. Slow, deep pools follow.

Just before mile 6, a major river right outside bend signals the start of some good fishing. Riffles, stone walls, and rocky debris characterize this bend. Coming out of this bend you will see cliffs on river right and more riffles. Slowly moving pools and shoreline abodes and a road next let you know that you are nearing the community of Millesons Mill on river left at mile 8. A large pool lies downstream and then you will enter a river right outside bend that features cliffs and riffles. A six-foot-tall rock wall also lies within and forms numerous micro-eddies. The next feature is a mid-river island, run it on its right. Soon you will come to the bridge that marks the Millesons Mill take-out.

15

MILLESONS MILL TO
INDIAN ROCK

U.S.G.S. QUAD:
Springfield, Levels, and Oldtown
DISTANCE:
8.75 miles
RAPIDS:
Riffles
ACCESS POINTS:
At Millesons Mill (Hampshire County), access is at the County Route 3 Bridge on river right (via Route 28) where there is a concrete ramp and parking. There is an alternative take-out 4.75 miles downstream at Blue Ford; the river left take-out is nothing but a sand beach off a dirt road via County Route 1-1 and County Route 1. Parking is limited. At Indian Rock (Hampshire County), there is a concrete ramp on river left off Arnold Stickley Road north via Route 1. Parking is available in a gravel parking lot.

A S THE TRIP begins, a heavily wooded mountainside character-izes the river left bank, and fields predominate on the opposite shore the first mile of this getaway. The river flows gently with only an occasional riffle and a lone islet. Through here, I once saw two Eastern kingbird males (I'm assuming the combatants were males—a safe assumption in the natural world) engage in an aerial battle in the middle

Tim Wimer takes time to fish near the Indian Rock access point.

of the river. After much flapping and uttering of alarm notes, the victor routed the interloper, which fled back to his side of the South Branch.

At mile 2, the river makes a quick, sharp turn and forms a small river right bend, but then straightens. A few riffles ensue before a lazy river left outside bend appears. Near mile 3, you will pass by an island; take the right route—you are at the beginning of an S curve that will take you to the Blue Ford take-out. The habitat and the smallmouth fishing are generally limited on this part of the float, probably making it the weakest section on the lower South Branch.

Riffles will send you coursing away from the access point, and you will note a heavily wooded river left shoreline on the first mile of this trip. Soon, though, fields will dominate both sides of the river and riffles will appear from time to time. At about one mile past the Blue Ford take-out, you will enter a mile-long river right outside bend that is heavily wooded. Linger here for some good fishing.

At mile 2 below Blue Ford, the river straightens and you will spot some homes and camps on river right, as well as a bluff. A large island then cleaves the river, and you can float down either side of it. Riffles lie below the island. You will next come to some eddies and water willow beds that speckle the waterway as the river creates a river left outside bend.

Only a mile of riffles and pools now are left before you come to the Indian Rock take-out. A large boulder on river left makes this access point aptly named and easy to spot.

PART III

THE UPPER POTOMAC (WEST VIRGINIA AND MARYLAND)

16

INDIAN ROCK TO PAW PAW

U.S.G.S QUADS:
Oldtown and Paw Paw

DISTANCE:
13½ miles

RAPIDS:
Class Is and riffles

ACCESS POINTS:
At Indian Rock (near Green Spring in Hampshire County), there is a con-crete ramp on river left off Arnold Stickley Road north via Route 1. Parking is available in a gravel parking lot. At Paw Paw (Morgan County, WV) just below the Route 9 Bridge, there is a concrete ramp on river right. Parking spaces are numerous in a paved parking lot.

THERE IS NO formal take-out at the confluence of the South Branch and North Branch. So I begin my coverage of the Main Stem with the last 4.5 miles of the South Branch. I first floated this section with friend Tim Wimer. Interestingly, not long after Wimer and I embarked on our trip, I caught a 7-inch smallmouth that the West Virginia DNR had tagged. Per the tag's instructions, I removed the tag and later sent it to the DNR office in Parkersburg. The data that I sent in, and hopefully that other anglers will submit if the opportunity arises, is one small way that we can help state fisheries manage the resource. The first half mile of this float is straight and flat, but then you come to a

You'll float under this bridge just above the confluence of the South and North Branches.

river left outside bend and some riffles. The next major feature is a series of cliffs on river left. Both offer fishing and photographic opportunities.

The river then slows and deepens and you will paddle through some deep water and enter a river right curve. Look for homes on the river right side. The South Branch straightens again and Stony Run enters on river right at about mile 2. I have found the smallmouth bass fishing through here mediocre, but the action for redbreast sunfish is good. Redbreasts are an underutilized game fish and certainly an attractive one, especially the males, which feature bright red breasts during the spawning season. The most enjoyable way, I think, to catch these sunfish is with a fly rod popper. The hits are violent, but the runs are short unless a fish happens to turn its rather large sides into the current and resistance builds up.

Next, the river forms a lazy river right bend, and you will spot more cliffs on river right. At about mile 4, an easy Class I is followed by another Class I that lies at a braided channel. This area is perhaps the best on the South Branch part of this float for smallies. Arnold Stickley Road follows the left side. Not long afterwards, you will pass under a railroad bridge and enter the confluence of the North Branch and the South Branch.

The first mile of the Main Stem Potomac features a great deal of shallow, rocky habitat with numerous water willow beds and a long Class I right above an island. It was through here, on that same float with Tim, that I thought I had caught my biggest ever Potomac smallmouth. I had cast a Rapala Original Minnow into the swift water and received a jarring strike. I immediately yelled to Tim that I had a trophy smallmouth on and begged him to maneuver the canoe so that I could concentrate on playing the bass.

For some two minutes, I played the fish, which dashed back and forth through the Class I. Finally, I brought the fish to the boat, and, to my shock, I had two 10-inch smallmouths on—one had attacked the front treble of the Rapala; the other, the rear one. It is true that I had landed 20 inches worth of smallmouths, and the reason for the great battle was because apparently each fish had decided to head in opposite directions. Tim understandably laughed and hooted at me. Frankly, the whole affair was one of the biggest disappointments I have ever had while fishing.

Next, the river flows fairly straight for the next 2 miles with the occasional riffle and with Town Creek entering on river left; at its juncture, you have paddled about 7 miles overall; next you will see an aqueduct. After the entrance of Town Creek, the next major feature is a series of riffles above and at an island; take the left passage. This is a good place to fish, as the smallies are drawn to the riffle. The hamlet of Okonoko lies in this area. The Main Stem lies in an isolated region through here as for the most part both banks are heavily wooded for the next several miles, especially the Maryland side on river left. Railroad tracks parallel the opposite bank on the West Virginia shore.

At about mile 10, the Little Cacapon enters on river right, and the river is deep through here. Yet another aqueduct lies at the confluence of the two rivers, as does the community of Little Cacapon. Next, you will come to a large island with passages on both sides possible, and another island lies directly below that offers good passage on both sides.

After paddling another mile, you will come to a lazy river right curve, and you now begin the final two miles of this float. You will float by one small island at the first part of this section, and for the most part the Potomac flows slowly. Soon you will come to the take-out on river right.

17

PAW PAW TO BONDS LANDING

U.S.G.S QUADS:
Paw Paw and Artemas

DISTANCE:
13½ miles

RAPIDS:
Class Is and riffles

ACCESS POINTS:
At Paw Paw (Morgan County, WV) just below the Route 9 Bridge, there is a concrete ramp on river right. Parking spaces are abundant in a paved parking lot. At Bonds Landing in the Green Ridge State Forest (Alleghany County, Maryland), there is a gravel ramp on river left. This ramp is not easy to travel to. Take a right at Oldtown Orleans Road Southeast, a left onto Carroll Road, and then a left onto Kesacamp Road and follow the sign. Parking is available.

MATT KNOTT OF River Riders in Harpers Ferry has paddled the entire upper Potomac except for the extreme white water of Great Falls and Little Falls and shares why he feels the river is so special. "One of the main reasons people come to this area of Maryland, West Virginia, and Virginia is the historical sites," said Knott. "But when you paddle much of the upper Potomac, the isolation is such that you could be a thousand miles from anywhere. Couple that with the fact that every five miles or so, the C&O Canal offers camping facilities on the Maryland side. It's really special to paddle up to a bank and spend the night there."

The Paw Paw Bends are one of the prettiest parts of the entire watershed.

The first six or so miles of this float offers some of the best smallmouth habitat on the entire Potomac Watershed. This is the area of the famous Paw Paw Bends, a series of curves where the river snakes through the surrounding countryside. In terms of trip planning, anglers should spend much of their time here. Pleasure boaters may want to stop often to take pictures of the wooded shorelines, railroad bridges, and of course the Main Stem. The bird watching for "woods" avians is outstanding through here, as such species as scarlet tanagers, red-eyed vireos, American redstarts, cardinals, Carolina wrens, and pileated, downy, and red-bellied woodpeckers are common.

Soon after you leave the ramp, you will enter the beginning of the Bends, a river right curve, which is immediately followed by a long riffle, Western Maryland Railroad Trestle 1, and a river left bend. Interestingly, the trestles in this section are all numbered.

After coming out of the river left bend, you pass under Trestle 2 and encounter another series of riffles at mile 3. Then comes a Class I rapid and yet another bend on river right. The Potomac straightens for a mile but then forms a Class I rock garden, which should be run on far river right, and then comes Trestle 3 around mile 5.

In about a mile, the river makes a river right bend and then comes a long section where shallow riffles predominate. In short order, you will then pass under Trestles 4 and 5. The tip of an island lies just above Trestle 5 and at about mile 9; take the right passageway for the most water. There is great fishing and scenery throughout.

The island stretches for nearly a mile, and then you will come to several small islands; take the left route by them. It is in this area that the C&O Canal once again runs along the Free State shore. Fishermen may want to camp here. Usually, I allot one hour of paddling time to fish one mile of river. But the habitat is so sublime through here that avid anglers may want to slow their pace. The Potomac next makes a long, lazy river left bend of some two miles. Soon after you will come to Trestle 6 and then Maryland's Green Ridge State Forest and the river left concrete ramp known as Bonds Landing. If I had to list my five favorite floats on the Main Stem, Paw Paw to Bonds Landing would definitely make the grade—easy to float and outstanding fishing, birding, and scenery.

18

BONDS LANDING TO LITTLE ORLEANS

U.S.G.S QUADS:
Paw Paw and Artemas

DISTANCE:
8½ miles

RAPIDS:
Riffles and Class Is

ACCESS POINTS:
At Bonds Landing in the Green Ridge State Forest, there is a gravel ramp on river left. This ramp is not easy to travel to. Take a right at Oldtown Orleans Road Southeast, a left onto Carroll Road, and then a left onto Kesacamp Road and follow the sign. Parking is available. At Little Orleans (Alleghany County, MD), there is a river left concrete ramp where Fifteen Mile Creek enters. The ramp is at the end of Little Orleans Road. Parking spaces are numerous in a gravel lot and a C&O campground is here.

AFTER PASSING BONDS Landing, you will drift through a section with deep, rocky pools followed by riffles. This is especially excellent wintertime habitat, and the riffle areas hold good numbers of smallies in the spring and summer. The Main Stem then forms a river right bend with the occasional riffle. Around mile 3, you will see some purplish bluffs on the West Virginia side.

Outside bends are excellent places to fish because they typically contain

The Bonds Landing float features plenty of campsites along the C&O Canal. Here Tim Wimer prepares breakfast.

deeper water as well as cover such as downed trees and rocks. During the warm weather months, by mid-morning smallies will have retreated to the deeper, shaded water found in outside bends. These fish often have fed heavily during the night and early morning hours, yet they can still be tempted by a topwater pattern such as the classic Sneaky Pete or a Walt's Popper. My friend Anthony Hipps of Lexington, North Carolina, makes an outstanding soft-bodied popper that also can draw savage surface strikes.

Anglers debate whether poppers should be dead drifted or enticingly wiggled so as to dimple the surface. Some folks even like to violently snap their poppers. Although I have come to believe that no method of fishing is ever always the only way to do something, I do think that dead drifting poppers is the way to start fishing a shaded outside bend. Some of the most tantalizing and ultimately exciting strikes I have ever experienced are when I have dead drifted poppers through a shaded outside bend and watched smallies slowly, oh so slowly, rise up and sip in my offering. Then the aerial acrobatics begin.

Next come a rocky, river right bank and some shallow, rocky water. Then you will drift past two islands (take the right passageway) and pass under Trestle 7 at mile 4. After another mile, you will enter a lazy river left bend that features plenty of rocky cover. For the next two miles, the Potomac flows gently and you will pass under Trestle 8. Paddlers and anglers may want to make time through here. Then you will pass by several houses on river right at what was once the hamlet of Doe Gully, course through a riffle, paddle through a sharp river right curve, and arrive at the Little Orleans ramp on river left.

19

LITTLE ORLEANS TO HANCOCK

U.S.G.S QUADS:
Paw Paw, Artemas, Great Cacapon, Bellegrove, and Hancock

DISTANCE:
17½ miles

RAPIDS:
Class Is and riffles

ACCESS POINTS:
At Little Orleans (Alleghany County, MD), there is a concrete ramp on river left where Fifteen Mile Creek enters. The ramp is at the end of Little Orleans Road. Parking spaces are numerous in a gravel lot and there is a C&O campground here. At Hancock (Washington County, MD), there is a concrete ramp on river left off Canal Street some 300 yards below the Route 522 Bridge. A paved parking lot is available.

AFTER YOU LEAVE Little Orleans, be prepared to fish some excellent habitat. As the river bends to the left, and then back to the right, riffles and underwater rock cover exist throughout these first two miles and the river left shoreline is heavily wooded. Next comes a river left curve at about mile 3, as well as some deep-water ledges in an area known as Turkey Foot Bend. With the C&O Canal running along river left, boaters have many choices for camping. In fact, Tim Wimer and I spent one night on this bank.

That night on the Main Stem. Tim and I had originally planned to

The Little Orleans float is yet another excursion that offers quality fishing.

camp at the Little Orleans access point, but when we arrived, others were there—they had apparently made the same decision we had. Seeking solitude, we floated downstream for several more miles before we saw an opening in the river left canopy along the C&O Canal—the Turkey Foot Bend area. Paddling over, we found a likely looking spot for me to pitch my tent and Tim to position his hammock. The evening was uneventful, but the nighttime sounds were glorious. A bull frog and a green frog began to belt out their mating calls, the former his well-known "ribbit," the latter his "twang," which sounds like it emanated from a banjo thus earning this amphibian his nickname: the banjo frog. After a while, the green frog gave up on attracting any females, but the bullfrog was relentless in his quest. I am a light sleeper and often awake several times every night. And each time I did so at the campsite, our bull frog was still appealing to those apparently uncooperative females.

Besides the pleasure gained from listening to the two species, I also found it delightful just to hear frogs. Wherever I go fishing these days, fewer frogs seem to be present. Many reasons why this is so have been proffered such as climate change, pollution, habitat loss, and introduced species. I have also noted similar declines in another water loving species, the painted turtle. Whereas in the past, I would spot numerous painted turtles along the Potomac Watershed, often basking on trees that had fallen into the water, I often only see one or two at a time now.

For the next 5 miles, the Potomac flows fairly straight. Sideling Hill Creek enters on river left (about 5 miles from the put-in), and some water willow covered islets appear. Just before mile 8, you will spot the remains of a dam; paddle on far river left. Shortly afterwards, you will spot an aqueduct and the Great Cacapon River entering on river right. Below the confluence lies some intriguing rocky cover on river right.

At about mile 9, the Potomac forms a river right bend, look for its rocky sections, followed by a Class I and then some slow water for a mile. At mile 12, Sir Johns Run enters on river right and fields dominate that shoreline. The river then makes a quick bend to the right and flows straight for about a mile with riffles interspersed. Next comes a river left bend in which lies a large rock formation. The Main Stem flows straight for less than a mile, then Grasshopper Hollow enters on river right; you will also see some cliffs in the area. All that is left now is a 2-mile fairly straight float to the take-out. You will float by a brick chimney and an aqueduct on river left. This area receives a great deal of fishing pressure from anglers in motorized johnboats.

The 522 bridge marks your take-out. Pass through a rock ledge and under the bridge and look for the ramp on river left. I recommend taking two days to fish this section, unless you are a run-and-gun type angler— that is someone who covers two miles per hour of fishing. For medium to advanced paddlers, this is a superb day trip.

20

HANCOCK TO MCCOYS FERRY

U.S.G.S QUADS:
Hancock, Cherry Run, and Big Pool

DISTANCE:
14 miles

RAPIDS:
Class Is and riffles

ACCESS POINTS:
At Hancock (Washington County), there is a concrete ramp on river left off Canal Street some 300 yards below the Route 522 Bridge. A paved parking lot is available. At McCoys Ferry (Washington County), there is a concrete ramp on river left off McCoy's Ferry Road via Route 56. Paddlers can also take-out at a river right concrete ramp at Cherry Hill on County Route 10 in Morgan County, 10 miles below Hancock. Parking is available in a paved lot. An alternative take-out is at Fort Frederick State Park on river left 12 miles below Hancock. The ramp is gravel and can be reached via Route 56 and Fort Frederick Road. Parking is available in a gravel lot.

MARYLAND DNR FISHERIES biologist John Mullican recommends that for fishermen the Hancock float is "a long way to paddle so skip the flat shallow sections and concentrate on the best habitat." Riverside camping is available at Fort Frederick State Park and McCoys Ferry, as well as the hiker/biker campsites on the C&O Canal along river left.

The Hancock ramp is often a busy place, so those anglers wanting to

Tim Wimer and Doak Harbison preparing to shove off from the Hancock access point.

travel to McCoys Ferry may find it prudent at the start of the trip to put some distance between them and the access point. The first mile features the odd riffle, water willow beds, and the entrances of Dry Run on river right and Tonoloway Creek on river left. Note the arch over the latter tributary.

Next comes a large island; the left side offers the best passageway and a riffle to Class I. The submerged rocky stretch above the island offers potential, especially in the early spring. And here's a fishing tidbit about the Potomac System. Of all the Mid-Atlantic rivers I have plied, no waterway offers the best "downstream of the island" action that this one does. Often on the South Branch and especially the Potomac, the current swirls and fish gather at the point below the tip of an island. A fast moving lure or a rapidly retrieved fly will often perform well.

For the next 3 to 4 miles, the Potomac flows fairly straight. From late spring through fall, expect to find lots of star grass in this area. I have caught 12- to 14-inch smallies in this vegetation. Indeed, the vegetation and habitat are both high quality in this float. Matt Knott, who operates

River Riders in Harpers Ferry, says that the Hancock float has much to offer. "There are a lot of riffles and no major rapids," Knott said. "The banks are mostly wooded with rolling hills in the background."

At mile 6, you'll come to a small island on your left and a much larger one to your right; go between them for the best and safest passageway. Riffles below the islands will send you on your way. And a local campground lies along the West Virginia shoreline. You'll also see where Sleepy Creek enters on river right.

At mile 7, you will encounter another island, which is nearly a mile long. Take the left passageway for the best fishing. This section features a bit of deep water and dropoffs—a good thing to know if you aim to take this float during the spring when deep diving crankbaits and Carolina rigs work so well for habitat such as this.

Around mile 8, a much smaller island comes into view. A power line also crosses here and Licking Creek soon enters on river left near more islands. For the next 2 miles, the Potomac flows fairly slowly; the major feature is the Cherry Hill ramp on river right, which is also where the namesake creek enters. A railroad trestle also helps mark this area.

The next 4 miles until the McCoys Ferry take-out has good fishing. A number of areas are 3 to 6 feet deep with riffles and submerged rocks. It was through one such area that I experienced one of my biggest ever fishing thrills while on a trip with Tim Wimer and Doak Harbison. I had been fan casting a 4-inch Cordell Red Fin through this type of rocky habitat when a 15-inch smallmouth attacked the lure.

Fortunately, and yes the word is *fortunately*, I lost the smallie after about 10 seconds and then proceeded to miss another 15-incher that likewise hit the hard plastic jerkbait on the same cast. But while I was moaning about my incompetence—and the Red Fin was slowly rising to the surface—yet another bronzeback blasted the bait.

I quickly felt that this bass was far bigger than the other two, as it commenced a searing run and I was forced to begin back reeling, as Doak Harbison expertly kept our canoe positioned parallel to where the fish was cavorting. When the bass first jumped, it was confirmed that I was dueling a real lunker—something that was hammered home each of the next three times that the smallie surfaced. Finally, I was able to land, take pictures, and release the 20-inch fish.

Between miles 12 and 13, you'll note where Back Creek enters on river right and Fort Frederick State Park lies on river left. At mile 14, you will see the McCoys Ferry takeout on river left.

21

MCCOYS FERRY TO FOUR LOCKS/DAM NO. 5

U.S.G.S QUADS:
Big Pool, Hedgesville, and Williamsport

DISTANCE:
8 miles

RAPIDS:
Riffles

ACCESS POINTS:
At McCoys Ferry (Washington County), there is a concrete ramp on river left off McCoy's Ferry Road via Route 56. Parking is available in a paved lot. At Four Locks (Washington County, MD) there is a concrete ramp on river left off Four Locks Road via Route 56. Parking is available.

MATT KNOTT OF River Riders describes this float as "miles of no current" and he is correct. Some scattered riffles appear for the first mile, but after that the backwaters of Dam 5 dominate. That first mile, though, can offer some quality smallmouth angling near ledges, water willow beds, and drop-offs.

After that first mile, you may be better off to target largemouth bass than smallmouth and to be in a motorized boat instead of a canoe. Indeed, canoeists and kayakers infrequently take this trip. Actually, the wintertime is probably one of the best times to use a powerboat on this section, as the scattered rocks on river left tend to concentrate bass.

You will have to portage on the McCoys Ferry float.

Those rocks are part of a four-mile long U-curve. At the bottom of the curve, you will float by the community of Little Georgetown. Generally, the river left shoreline is heavily wooded and farmland, campers, fields, and houses characterize the Mountain State side. A cliff marks the approach of the Four Locks ramp on river left. Two more miles of lake-style paddling through a river left bend will take you to Dam No. 5. You will need to debark when you come to the buoys and danger sign warning of the dam downstream. I recommend portaging on the left side.

The focus of this book is fishing for river smallmouth, paddling recreationally, birding, and taking pictures. I have taken this trip one time and will never take it again, as this excursion has little to offer those user groups. However, I do have one little tidbit of knowledge to impart. On that sole trip while with Doak Harbison and Tim Weimer, I began to hear the call notes of yellow-billed cuckoos ("coo-coo-coo," then repeat) and the trilling of a gray tree frog. I have long associated these sounds with an imminent thunderstorm and such was the case that day. If you hear these two creatures and the sky begins to darken, my advice is to stop paddling and seek shelter.

22

FOUR LOCKS TO WILLIAMSPORT

U.S.G.S. QUADS:
Hedgesville and Williamsport

DISTANCE:
8 miles

RAPIDS:
Class Is and riffles

ACCESS POINTS:
At Four Locks (Washington County, MD), there is a concrete ramp on river left off Four Locks Road via Route 56. Parking is available. At Williamsport (Washington County, MD) there is a concrete ramp on river left at River Bottom Park via Salisbury Street. Parking is available in a gravel lot.

SINCE DOAK HARBISON and I were in a canoe and Tim Wimer in a kayak, and since we were on a three-day voyage on this particular outing, we obviously opted not to debark from the river at Four Locks and quickly paddled the 2 miles from there to Dam No. 5. As you near the structure, you'll see the obligatory "Danger Dam Downstream" warning, as well as buoys indicating the dam's proximity. The best portage is on river left, and you can put back in just below the dam and above some islands covered with water willow.

The 6-mile section below Dam No. 5 has much to recommend it. Good numbers of smallmouths, and some nice size ones, dwell throughout and the habitat is superb. After you work the islands below the structure,

Tim Wimer with a nice smallie caught on the Four Locks excursion.

some swiftly flowing riffles and gentle Class Is will send you downstream. A little over a mile below the dam, you'll come to a series of large islands that extend for approximately a mile. The best passageway is down their right sides. This entire area is a great place to work crankbaits and streamers and if the topwater bite is on, surface lures and flyrod poppers. At the end of these islands, an old bridge support serves as a landmark and a quarry is also in the area on river right. There are lots of submerged rocks. Numerous water willow beds, dropoffs, and cuts lie within these islands and offer marvelous mossyback potential. You also may be able to glimpse where a river right spring enters.

A river left outside curve (known as Millers Bend) characterizes the next 2 miles with a cliff on river right at the beginning of the bend and a stonewall lying in its heart. This is a scenic section with wooded shorelines, and the smallie sport remains top-notch. In the spring and summer, this area is a wonderful place to work slowly sinking soft plastic jerkbaits through the water column. The next major feature is a quarry on river left and the rocky pools and riffles continue to provide angling opportunities.

The quarry ends about a mile above the Williamsport ramp, and the river slows considerably below the quarry. During the warm weather period, expect to see vast fields of star grass throughout this section. Streamers and buzzbaits are excellent lures and can result in some violent hits if the topwater bite is on. A half mile or so above Williamsport, you'll drift by Duck Island, which is soon followed by another island as the Potomac makes a gentle turn. Below these islands, figure to observe a number of wade and bank fishermen as well as pleasure boaters and anglers motoring upstream from the launch.

Right before the take-out, you'll see Conococheague Creek enter on river left and you'll paddle under the Route 11 bridge.

23

WILLIAMSPORT TO DAM NO. 4

U.S.G.S. QUADS:
Williamsport
DISTANCE:
15 miles
RAPIDS:
Class I and riffles
ACCESS POINTS:
At Williamsport (Washington County, MD), there is a concrete ramp on river left at River Bottom Park via Salisbury Street. Parking is available in a gravel lot. Above Dam No. 4 (Washington County, MD), a river left paved ramp lies off Dam No. 4 Road via Route 63. Parking is available.

T HE FIRST ORDER of business is to portage on river left around the Pepco power plant dam. This is not a long portage as such things go and takes only about 15 minutes. On a float with fellow school teachers Doak Harbison and Tim Wimer, we saw some high school boys swimming below the dam, and we teachers are told never to miss what is called "a teaching moment." I approached the young folks, identified myself as a high-school English teacher of grades nine and ten, and asked them what books they had read in those classes. I would have thought that the last thing those boys would have wanted to discuss on a hot summer day was English 9 and 10 literature, but they and I engaged in a spirited three-minute conversation on the positives and negatives

Doak Harbison landed this smallie at the beginning of the Williamsport getaway.

of *Call of the Wild*, *Animal Farm*, and *Romeo and Juliet* for English 9 and *Of Mice and Men* and *Hamlet* for English 10. Doak and Tim waited patiently for me to finish my English lesson, and we then moved on, but not before I gave the boys some fishing lures as thanks for tolerating a teacher when school was closed for the summer.

Below the dam, numerous riffles, eddies, and water willow islets exist, and we found the smallmouths abundant. During the spring, this is a good place to work nymphs and grubs, and buzzbaits and streamers are effective in the summer. The Potomac flows straight through here, and power lines and the Interstate 81 bridge are within sight.

Indeed, the first 2 miles of this float are straight and feature similar habitat. At the end of this stretch, you will pass under a railroad bridge at the start of Powell Bend (which forms a gentle river left curve) and then float by some manmade islands and remains of old railroad trestles. Then you will notice a solid slate-like bottom that offers poor habitat. This is an interesting and unique stream bottom. I can't think of anywhere else on the South Branch and Main Stem that looks like this does. Next is a Class I rapid, which you'll want to run down the middle.

For about a mile past the rapid, you can still have some good fishing for smallies near star grass fields. But then the backwaters of Dam No. 4 truly begin and you will be faced with the chore of paddling over 11 miles of slow, deep water. Doak, Tim, and I undertook this excursion because we wanted the experience of paddling the entire upper Potomac in West Virginia. However, this portion is nothing more than a lake.

To briefly let you know what is in store, the river forms a river right bend some 5 miles below the put-in, and homes and docks become increasingly more common. The river then flows fairly straight for several more miles, and you will note where Opequon Creek enters on river right as the river forms a river right curve, which is followed, a mile later, by a left curve.

Then some 12 miles below the launch, you'll come to a left curve and some cliffs on that side. In this area, if you take time to debark for a few minutes, you can observe McMahon's Mill and a small creek that runs into the river. At this point of our excursion, we were all fatigued, having paddled 25 miles that day. Doak and Tim were both suffering from heat exhaustion, and it was late on a blistering hot evening. We had planned to camp at McMahon's Mill on the C&O Canal but found that doing so was prohibited.

Knowing that my buddies could travel no further, I paddled across to the West Virginia side and began knocking on the doors of lakeside homes and trailers, inquiring if we could spend the night camping on someone's property. It was there that I met Mike and Christie Masters who kindly gave us permission to pitch a tent in their front yard.

As an English teacher and travel writer, one of my favorite quotes is from Tennessee Williams' play, *A Streetcar Named Desire*, which states: "I have always depended on the kindness of strangers." After retrieving Doak and Tim and beginning the process of setting up a tent, I remarked to Mike that I had brought some venison steaks to cook over a fire, that I would not, of course, build a fire in his front yard, and would he like the venison as a token of our appreciation?

Mike heartily laughed and said that we could use his outdoor grill to cook the steak and that he, in fact, would prepare the meat for us. To our joy and surprise, as soon as the steak was finished, Christie brought us heaping plates of garlic mashed potatoes and corn, as well as offered us our choice of soft drinks or bottled water. We were overwhelmed by the generosity of the Masters. Again, I've always depended on the kindness of strangers.

Refreshed, the next morning we quickly paddled the 2½ miles or so to Dam 4 and undertook a portage of some 30 minutes on river left around it.

24

DAM NO.4 TO TAYLORS LANDING

U.S.G.S. QUADS:
Williamsport and Shepherdstown

DISTANCE:
3.5 miles

RAPIDS:
Class I and riffles

ACCESS POINTS:
There are no public access point below the dam. Above Dam No. 4 (Washington County, MD), a river left paved ramp lies off Dam No. 4 Road via Route 63. Parking is available. You will have to portage around the dam to begin your float. At Taylors Landing (Washington County, MD), two river left concrete ramps exist; take the upper one above a rapid. The ramps are located off Taylors Landing Road via Fair Play Road. Parking is available in a paved lot.

IMMEDIATELY BELOW THE dam, the quality habitat begins and extends throughout the trip. Slicks, boils, riffles, and water willow beds characterize the first mile or so of the float. A rocky river left shoreline lies above the first major feature, Shepherds Island, which is really two long land masses. Take the left passageway for the best water depth, and the riffles will help send you along your way. As one would expect, the habitat throughout is superlative with swift water and a rocky substrate. When you come to the end of the island, you will have covered about 2 miles. Anglers should plan to spend a great deal of time here

The Dam No. 4 to Taylors Landing float is a favorite of the author.

while paddlers will enjoy the brisk pace, and both will find the scenery pleasing. Additionally, the islands often attract great blue and green herons and a host of songbirds.

Next come a set of riffles, which are followed by a Class I; run it on far river left. In this general area, you will also soon see a cliff on the right bank, which is heavily wooded. The river then forms a river left bend, and more riffles ensue. Star grass thrives in this section during the summer and provides more habitat for bronzebacks. Soon afterwards you'll come to Taylors Landing.

I have tried to add tidbits of helpful information regarding floating the Potomac and here's another suggestion. Please avoid wearing cotton clothing. I know that cotton is light and cool, but if the weather turns colder and cotton clothing becomes wet, hypothermia is a worst case scenario and misery is the best case one. I must confess that on one excursion down this river with Tim Wimer and Doak Harbison, I brought along light cotton long johns to sleep in when we pitched camp. One morning while in the process of sealing my dry bag, I carelessly left part of the bag open.

During our day on the river, somehow or another water entered the bag, and that evening when I went to change into the "cotton pajamas" they were waterlogged. And they never dried out during that particular three-day float—another negative trait of cotton is that it retains moisture. Tim teased me unmercifully about my cotton pajamas, and I felt stupid to have brought them.

25

TAYLORS LANDING TO
SNYDERS LANDING

U.S.G.S. QUAD:
Shepherdstown

DISTANCE:
4.5 miles

RAPIDS:
Riffles and Class Is

ACCESS POINTS:
At Taylors Landing (Washington County, MD), there are two river left concrete ramps; take the lower one below a rapid. The ramps are located off Taylors Landing Road via Fair Play Road. Parking is available in a paved lot. At Snyders Landing (Washington County, MD), there is a concrete ramp on river left off Snyders Landing Road via Route 34. Parking is available in a large paved lot.

THIS IS ONE of the most delightful floats on the upper Potomac. I have taken this trip many times, and truly every single time have caught quality smallmouth bass. In fact, I would rate it as one of the best on the entire South Branch and Main Stem. At the beginning, a Class I ledge lies to the right of the two ramps. If you are coming straight through from Dam 4, you can scoot down the right side of this rapid. If not, merely launch from the lower ramp.

Maryland Department of Natural Resources biologist John Mullican

Doak Harbison was angling for smallmouth on the Taylors Landing trip when this catfish hit.

says that Dam No. 4 to Taylors Landing and Taylors to Snyders both have excellent habitat for smallmouth throughout and many opportunities to wade during summer low flows. Through this float, the water clips along over a rocky substrate with scattered water willow beds and generous helpings of deep water ledges and star grass fields.

At the beginning of the float, which lies in a river left bend, you will course through numerous riffles and by water willow beds on that curve. When you enter a straight stretch below the bend, you will note more grass beds as well as lots of rocks along the left shoreline. This mile-long straight stretch features numerous ledges and riffles as well as the occasional drop that can become a Class I in high water.

Two miles below the lower ramp you will enter a river right curve (known as Horseshoe Bend) and yet more ledges. Here is another locale where I have enjoyed solid smallie success over the years. Once you leave that bend, more eddies and water willow beds mark the Potomac and the Potomac flows fairly straight until you arrive at Snyders Landing. Both banks are heavily wooded, and the right one offers both wood and rock cover. In the preface, I stated that anglers should generally allot one hour of fishing time per one mile of river covered. This is one of those floats that it might be better to allot two hours per mile.

Since this is such an outstanding fishing float, I wanted to close with some angling tips. When I give seminars, I often am asked about rod selection and which is my favorite. I try not to have favorite rods of any kind. For example, my ideal lineup is one medium heavy baitcaster, three spinning rods (two medium heavy and one medium) and one 8½-foot fly rod loaded with a 7- or 8-weight bass bug taper. If the smallmouths are holding deep, I can slug it out with them on the bottom with the baitcaster. The two medium heavy spinning outfits can be used for any number of lures such as spinnerbaits, tubes, and soft plastic jerkbaits. The medium action outfit is great for topwaters. And when finesse fishing is required, such as dead-drifting poppers beneath shoreline vegetation and in clear water, the fly rod excels. Many anglers are purists about their rods—some refuse to employ or take the time to learn how to use baitcasters, some spin fishermen shun fly rods, and some fly fishermen won't stoop to use a spinning rod. I would rather catch fish.

26

SNYDERS LANDING TO SHEPHERDSTOWN

U.S.G.S. QUAD:
Shepherdstown

DISTANCE:
4 miles

RAPIDS:
Riffles

ACCESS POINTS:
At Snyders Landing (Washington County, MD), there is a concrete ramp on river left off Snyders Landing Road via Route 34. Parking is available in a large paved lot. At Shepherdstown (Jefferson County, WV), there is a steep concrete ramp on river right off Princess Street. Limited parking is available in a paved lot.

T HE SNYDERS LANDING trip begins at the end of a curve known as Horseshoe Bend and a short, river left outside bend then immediately forms. Rocky cover is scattered about. I have taken this trip a number of times and rank it as one of my favorites on the Potomac. As a whole, the Snyders Landing float lacks major rapids, but what it does have in its favor are numerous boils, riffles, deep-water ledges, submerged rock piles, and water willow beds. This float can have some great fishing, especially in the spring and early to mid summer.

After the bend, the Potomac flows straight for almost a mile before

The Snyders Landing float features quality habitat.

curving river right. Widely scattered rocks lie along the shoreline and there is plenty of underwater structure. The Potomac then straightens, and flows over a series of submerged rock ledges and riffles before a short river left outside bend followed by more submerged ledges and riffles in the next straightaway.

You will next come through a short river right curve and view the Bavarian Inn high on the river right bank and then the James Rumsey Route 34 Bridge, followed by the remains of bridge supports, and the Shepherdstown ramp. A small creek further marks the ramp. Shepherdstown is a wonderful place to visit, and a great place to spend the night is the Shepherdstown Inn where Jeanne Muir and her husband, Jim Ford, will regale you with stories of the Battle of Antietam (which took place just across the river in Maryland and is known as the bloodiest battle of the Civil War) as well as the history of James Rumsey, who designed the Patowomack Canal.

27

SHEPHERDSTOWN TO DARGAN BEND

U.S.G.S. QUADS:
Shepherdstown, Keedysville

DISTANCE:
8 miles

RAPIDS:
Riffles

ACCESS POINTS:
At Shepherdstown (Jefferson County, WV), there is a steep concrete ramp on river right off Princess Street. Limited parking is available in a paved lot. At Dargan Bend (Washington County, MD), the river left take-out is a concrete ramp off Back Road via Harpers Ferry Road. Parking spaces are numerous.

THE FIRST TIME I undertook this float was with James Apperson, who operates Bass River Outfitters. Interestingly, the guide states that this is one of the best floats for smallmouth bass and channel catfish and that the cats often top 20 inches, especially if anglers go after them during low-light conditions or at night. Matt Knott, who operates River Riders, relates that the Shepherdstown excursion has a reputation for producing lots of 12- to 15-inch bronzebacks.

You will see plenty of landmarks near the Shepherdstown ramp: the James Rumsey Bridge, the remains of another structure, and a railroad

James Rumsey Bridge over the Potomac River at Shepherdstown. Ron Cogswell photo

bridge. On the float with Apperson, I guessed that the smallies might be in a chasing mood and so opted for a Big O crankbait. The fish hit this lure so steadily that I never took it off the entire outing. The first mile of this float consists of scattered riffles with sycamores and box elders crowding the river left shoreline along which the C&O Canal, of course, continues to run.

Packhorse Ford begins the second mile of the Shepherdstown getaway. According to Jeanne Muir, the shallow water here served as a major ford for both Confederate and Union soldiers. Below this shallow area come a series of riffles, each of which can hold numerous smallmouth bass. You will also start to spot a number of homes on river right. The river flows fairly straight through here and this tendency continues at the start of the third mile. Then, however, a series of underwater ledges periodically occur and these are always worth prospecting.

After you have gone three miles, the river bends slightly and you will next see Knott Island. The only real option is to float down its left side. Rattlesnake Run dribbles in on the right side of the island. Numerous silver maples crowd the river left bank, and these create some streamside cover, although not as good fish habitat as sycamores.

The next major feature is where Antietam Creek enters on river left, just before mile 4. An absolutely gorgeous aqueduct serves as a landmark. On a trip with Doak Harbison and Tim Wimer, we visited the Antietam Battlefield. As a history teacher, Doak was especially excited about seeing what has been called the single bloodiest day in American history as some 23,000 casualties occurred on September 17, 1862. Following a tour guide through the battlefield was an emotional experience for the three of us. When floating past the creek's entrance, I recalled that the stream was said to have flowed red with blood on that infamous day.

Soon afterwards come two major ledges, and the riffles and swift water in this area offer more outstanding fishing. After you have paddled about 6 miles from the put-in, the river forms a long, pronounced river right outside bend. This outside bend features numerous places to fish from small points to sycamore root wads to riffles and rocky cover. The bend concludes with yet another major riffle at about mile 7.5. Below here the river slows dramatically, and Dargan Bend lies a half mile or so downstream.

28

DARGAN BEND TO POTOMAC WAYSIDE

U.S.G.S. QUADS:
Keedysville, Harpers Ferry

DISTANCE:
5 miles

RAPIDS:
Riffles, Class Is, IIs, and IIIs

ACCESS POINTS:
At Dargan Bend (Washington County, MD), a concrete ramp on river left off Back Road via Harpers Ferry Road provides access. Parking spaces are numerous. At Potomac Wayside (Loudoun County, VA), the river right take-out is nothing more than a dirt incline off Route 340. Parking is limited at roadside pull-offs. Another informal dirt access point known as Sandy Hook is on the Maryland side under the Route 340 Bridge via Sandy Hook Road. Parking is limited. Note: a West Virginia or Maryland fishing license is required until you reach the confluence of the Shenandoah and Potomac, a Virginia or Maryland license afterwards.

THIS FLOAT SHOULD not be attempted except by expert paddlers as there are some rough and potentially dangerous rapids. Nevertheless, the river flows slowly for a little over 2½ miles to Dam No. 3, and the summertime boat traffic is intense, making it unpleasant for canoeists and kayakers. At the start of the trip, the Potomac flows

Lots of quality smallies fin The Needles on the Dargan Bend float.

straight and then forms a river right bend; at the end of the bend are the remains of Dam No. 3. Some individuals run the dam in kayaks or white water canoes. I do not recommend running the dam in any kind of craft because there is a considerable drop with possible debris below.

I recommend portaging on river left via the C&O Canal. Once you put back in below the dam, you will immediately enter The Needles section, which extends a little over 1½ miles. I have fished The Needles a number of times. In late summer, riffles predominate with the occasional Class I. In spring, those Class Is can become Class IIs in high water, and because of the many rapids, novice and even intermediate paddlers could experience trouble. This can be an outstanding area to fish, but please be aware that both the angling and pleasure boating traffic can be intense in the summer.

The Needles end where the Shenandoah River enters the Potomac. This is one of the most stunningly beautiful sections anywhere—the view that Thomas Jefferson described as "worth a trip across the Atlantic." Our third president spoke those words high on the Virginia hillside at what today is appropriately called "Jefferson's Rock." Part of that beauty can be seen in the major rapids that pock the Potomac after the Shenandoah commingles with it.

After the confluence, it is about .7 mile to the take-out. First, you will pass through an easy Class I, but then the bottom seems to drop out of the Main Stem. Class I to II Wakeup extends across much of the waterway and should be run on river left. Then Class III-plus White Horse looms with the most intense side on the left and dangerous hydraulics in its center. Portage on river left. Next is the Class III Washing Machine, which most people run on the far left. Again, I recommend that you not run either of these Class IIIs and portage along the C&O Canal. Next note where Piney Run enters on river right, and look for the sign announcing that you have arrived at the Potomac Wayside.

PART IV

THE UPPER POTOMAC (VIRGINIA AND MARYLAND)

29

POTOMAC WAYSIDE
TO **BRUNSWICK**

U.S.G.S. QUAD:
Harpers Ferry

DISTANCE:
5 miles

RAPIDS:
Riffles, Class Is, and IIs

ACCESS POINTS:
At Potomac Wayside (Loudoun County, VA), the river right take-out is nothing more than a dirt incline off Route 340. Parking is limited at roadside pull-offs. Another informal dirt access point known as Sandy Hook is on the Maryland side under the Route 340 bridge via Sandy Hook Road. Parking is limited. At the Brunswick Route 17 bridge (Frederick County, MD), there is a concrete ramp on river left off Maple Street via Maryland 17 (Burkittsville Road). Parking spaces are numerous in a paved lot.

THIS IS YET another outstanding float for anglers and paddlers. After launching, the first task is to move to the left side of what will become a long series of islands that extend for a mile or more. In general, the left side provides the best water, but anglers can dart in and out of both sides of the islets and fish any number of cuts, riffles, points, eddies, and current breaks. Paddlers and bird watchers will enjoy exploring these land masses; expect to see great blue and green

Poppers and other patterns will produce on the Potomac Wayside getaway.

herons, Canada geese, mallards, and maybe even some wood ducks. Bald eagles are a possibility as well.

Just before mile 2, you will enter a river left bend (the community of Weverton is on river left) and encounter three consecutive Class II rapids: Weverton Rapids (run on the right), File Factory (down the center), and Knoxville Falls (left side). In high water and/or in the spring, these rapids could be roaring along at a Class III pace. Please consider portaging along the C&O Canal on river left. Because of the rapids, only one person at a time can safely fish from a canoe, making this an ideal trip to take with a guide rowing a raft.

Next you will see a large island along the Maryland side, some islets, and a good size land mass toward the Virginia side. Fishing for small-mouth can be outstanding and the scenery is beautiful. You leave the tip of the island on the Maryland side about three miles from the put-in. Next comes a fairly straight stretch of about a mile, then you will come to three large islands. Good underwater rock cover here begs to be investigated with crankbaits and weighted streamers and nymphs.

After you pass the second large island, hug the river left side and shimmy through the left side of the third island toward the take-out under the Route 17 bridge.

30

BRUNSWICK to LANDER

U.S.G.S. QUADS:
Harpers Ferry, Point of Rocks

DISTANCE:
4 miles

RAPIDS:
Riffles, Class Is

ACCESS POINTS:
At the Brunswick Route 17 bridge (Frederick County, MD), there is a concrete ramp on river left off Maple Street via Maryland 17 (Burkittsville Road). Parking spaces are numerous in a paved lot. At Lander (Frederick County, MD), you can put in on river left off Lander Road via Route 340. Parking is limited.

O BEGIN YOUR float, you will have to paddle through a narrow passageway to reach the Main Stem. Don't let that little bit of maneuvering discourage you because the good fishing and birding begins immediately. In fact, the first time I took this float I caught a fine smallie on my initial cast of the day. The bass smashed a Cordell Big O, one of the best crankbaits ever.

The first two miles of this trip flow gently with the occasional ledge, water willow covered islet, elodea bed, and star grass stretches. Quarter Branch dribbles in on river right at about the 1.5-mile point. These two miles present excellent opportunities for fan casting crankbaits such as

The author with a fine smallmouth he caught on the Brunswick float.

Bomber Model As and Bandits, as well as streamers and Stimulators with the long rod. You can fish to some fair bank cover (mostly in the form of scattered sycamores and box elders) but the best action is mid river.

Riffles throughout occasionally metamorphose into Class I rapids, but the intermediate paddler will not find them overly difficult to run. Just past mile 3, the river forms a river left curve, a Class I ledge looms, and Catoctin Creek enters on river left. An island marks where the creek enters, and the Lander access point lies within the bend.

31

LANDER TO POINT OF ROCKS

U.S.G.S. QUADS:
Harpers Ferry, Point of Rocks

DISTANCE:
2½ miles

RAPIDS:
Riffles and easy Class Is

ACCESS POINTS:
At Lander (Frederick County, MD), there is a river left put-in off Lander Road via Route 340. Parking is available. At Point of Rocks (Frederick County, MD and Loudoun County, VA), access points exist at both sides of the river at the Route 15 bridge. On the Virginia side, Lovettsville Road leads to the river right access point where there is a concrete ramp and parking. There is also a concrete ramp on the Maryland side, just off Canal Road. Parking is available in a large lot.

ONE OF THE times I took this excursion was with guide James Apperson. James is an expert on catching quality catfish, especially jumbo channel cats, and he shared his tips with me. During the summer, he prefers to fish at night and concentrates on gravel bars where these predators have come to forage under cover of darkness. His bait of choice is a live 4- to 8-inch chub, attached to a circle hook. One of the most interesting aspects of James' strategy is that he employs relatively light line (8-pound-test) so that the chubs remain lively. A medium heavy spinning rod rounds out his gear.

Lander is yet another float that contains lots of smallie habitat.

Apperson also excels at catching cats during the day, when he targets dropoffs that lead to deep water, especially those near wood cover. Indeed, on our float, I caught a 20-inch channel that was holding on the end of a submerged log next to a dropoff. The cat hit a Big O crankbait. Obviously, I was angling for smallies, but I don't mind temporarily ceasing the chase for my favorite fish to tangle with a fat cat. On that same float, I tallied an incredible 51 species of birds, anchored, by of all things, a common loon. Among the other quality sightings were a bald eagle, great-crested flycatcher, belted kingfisher, and red-tailed hawk. Oh, by the way, I also landed a 15-inch smallie that likewise engulfed the Big O. The fishing and birding made for a memorable day.

The best approach on that day and many days on the Lander float is to work the elodea and water willow beds on or along the many islands, plus probe the downstream points of any land mass. A power line crosses the river just below the put-in and runs toward a campsite on the C&O Canal. An island lies in this area as well. Lots of vegetation and rocky cover lie along both sides of this island. James prefers the right side.

At mile 1, you'll arrive at a long chain of islands (the longest of which is Paton Island) and this type of island/riffle habitat occurs the rest of the trip. Apperson recommends working the left side of Paton and the island above it. After you drift by the end of Paton Island, you will spot the Route 15 bridge. You can take out on either side, depending on where you want to drive later. Although this float is short, the fishing spots are numerous and anglers could easily spend a full day probing all the quality spots.

32

POINT OF ROCKS TO NOLANDS FERRY

U.S.G.S. QUADS:
Point of Rocks, Buckeystown

DISTANCE:
3½ miles

RAPIDS:
Riffles

ACCESS POINTS:
At Point of Rocks (Frederick County, MD and Loudoun County, VA), access points exist at both sides of the river at the Route 15 Bridge. On the Virginia side, Lovettsville Road leads to the river right access point where there is a concrete ramp and parking in a gravel lot. There is also a concrete ramp on the Maryland side, just off Canal Road. Parking is available in a large gravel lot. At Nolands Ferry (Frederick County, MD), there is a concrete ramp on river left off Nolands Ferry Road via Tuscarora Road and limited parking in a paved lot.

THE POINT OF Rocks trip is short and delightful in terms of fishing, exploring, paddling, and photography. Soon after you put in, you will come to a small island to the left of a major landmass, Heaters Island, that runs for some 1½ miles. Probe the islet first then continue on down the left side of Heaters. All kinds of rocky cover, water willow, elodea beds, cuts, and boils exist here and the fishing can be fabulous.

Tim Wimer fishing on the Point of Rocks trip.

And as always on the Potomac, don't forget to work the points at the ends of islands. On one float past Heaters, I lost a fine 18-inch smallmouth that threw my plug on its third leap. It always hurts to lose any good-size smallie, but having such a fine fish escape is, unfortunately, hard to forget.

While working on this book, I gave a book signing for my other river guides and had a gentleman come up to me and state that he really liked how I always wrote about my mistakes. And I surely made some miscues playing the aforementioned smallie. From the time it struck, I felt that I had no control over the fish as it charged toward the boat, causing slack to form, then began its leaping exhibition. When the fish first went deep, I should have reset the hook, but I did not, which probably was the reason I lost it. Because of that lapse, when the smallie commenced jumping, it was only a matter of time before it became unhinged from the lure. When playing a leaping fish, you should thrust the rod downward to try to keep the fish below the surface.

Next comes Mason Island, which lies hard by the river right shore. The passage along this shore is narrow, so take the left side of the island.

The habitat along Mason Island, although okay, pales in comparison to that along Heaters. Immediately after you pass the tip of Mason Island, at mile 3, Noland Island arrives on the scene. Guide Ed Shelley of River Riders recommends that folks take the left side along Nolands Island.

Eddies and ledges lie along a small island to the left of Nolands; if fishing, explore this area first. Then scoot along the island and work more superb smallie hot spots, especially the water willow beds. About half way down this island you will come to the Nolands Ferry take-out.

33

NOLANDS FERRY TO
MOUTH OF MONOCACY

U.S.G.S. QUADS:
Buckeystown, Poolesville

DISTANCE:
3 miles

RAPIDS:
Riffles

ACCESS POINTS:
At Nolands Ferry (Frederick County, MD), there is a concrete ramp on river left off Nolands Ferry Road via Tuscarora Road. Parking is limited in a paved lot. At Mouth of Monocacy (Frederick County, MD), there is a concrete ramp on river left off Canal Road via Commerce Street. The ramp lies a short distance up from the river's mouth. Parking spaces are numerous in a paved lot.

THE NOLANDS FERRY float features outstanding action along its islands. After you launch from just inside the Monocacy River, you will drift into the Main Stem and paddle past Nolands Island. While on a trip with Ed Shelley of River Riders, he caught a 15-inch smallmouth (water willow beds, points, and bars add fishy features to the island) from along Nolands. The fish fell for a ⅛-ounce in-line spinner—which leads to an interesting point. I believe that the vast

Nolands Ferry is known for producing quality smallies like this one that Tim Wimer caught.

majority of time, the axiom about bigger bass wanting bigger baits is accurate, but not all the time.

Before our trip began, Ed told me that he had enjoyed outstanding success on the upper Potomac fishing spinners. He even asked me if I would like to borrow one of his. I politely declined, feeling that spinners are superb lures for rock bass and red-breast sunfish but not jumbo bronze-backs. Ed outfished me that day.

After you drift beyond Nolands Island, you will spot Meadow Island tight to the river right shoreline with Birdsaw Island downstream and to the left of it. Birdsaw Island actually has been cut in half by the forces of time, and this entire area (by that I mean both sides of Birdsaw and the cut between the two island components) is worth a great deal of your angling time. On a float through here with Tim Wimer, he pointed out a bald eagle cruising over Birdsaw.

At the tip of the bottom half of Birdsaw lies Cox Island, and both sides of Cox sport good cover as well. At the tip of Cox Island begins a stretch of flat, uninteresting water and soon you will see the Monocacy River Aqueduct on river left. Paddle upstream into the Monocacy a short distance to the take-out. Remember that either a Virginia or Maryland license is legal for the Main Stem beyond the confluence of the Shenandoah and Potomac. But if you decide to fish while maneuvering upstream on the Monocacy, you will need a Free State license.

34

MOUTH OF MONOCACY
TO **WHITES FERRY**

U.S.G.S. QUADS:
Poolesville, Waterford

DISTANCE:
6½ miles

RAPIDS:
Riffles, Class I

ACCESS POINTS:
At Mouth of Monocacy (Frederick County, MD), there is a concrete ramp on river left off Canal Road via Commerce Street. The ramp lies a short distance up from the river's mouth. Parking spaces are numerous in a paved lot. At Whites Ferry (Montgomery County, MD), there is a concrete ramp on river left off Whites Ferry Road via MD Route 28. Parking spaces are numerous in a large lot, for a fee.

A FTER YOU LEAVE the Monocacy River entrance, the Main Stem flows fairly straight for 1½ miles through fairly typical small-mouth habitat of scattered riffles and water willow beds; there is only a little rock cover. The only landmark of sorts is where the Little Monocacy enters on river left not far below where its bigger namesake enters. The next landmark is one you'll have no trouble spotting. The community of Dickerson lies on river left and a power plant on that same side releases its discharge at about 1¾ miles from the put-in. The

"Nighttime Parking" at a C&O Campsite below where the Monocacy River enters.

discharge picks up speed as it nears the Potomac creating an artificial Class I rapid.

That water is also warm, making the area downstream on river left a common wintertime destination for anglers seeking walleyes, catfish, and smallmouths, though when combined with summer temperatures, it makes the river left shoreline a poor place to fish for a distance downstream.

The next major landmark is Mason Island, about 3 miles downstream from the Monocacy. This is a massive island in length (some 2½ miles) and width in places (the bottom and wider ⅔ of the land mass is separated from the upper ⅓). A C&O Campsite across from where the two islands split is a nice place to stay. Doak Harbison, Tim Wimer, and I once spent a pleasant night there. On the way to the campsite, we saw a golden eagle and caught a number of 12- to 15-inch smallmouths by tossing Rapala Original Minnows to the abundant water willow beds, riffles, and rocky cover.

As I've noted before in this book, the campsites along the C&O Canal really enhance the experience of exploring the Main Stem. Many sites also feature running water and a fire pit. During my party's sojourn, several sisters arrived at the campsite, and in the course of conversation I came to ask them why they had come to the river. One sister was from New Jersey, the other from Virginia, and they had wanted to enjoy some time to catch up with what was going on with their respective lives. While I was chatting with the sisters, several Maryland folks who were biking the canal arrived at the campsite, but seeing two groups already there, moved on. That's another great thing about the canal; another campsite is not too far away.

I write often about my snafus, too often it seems sometimes—but there seem to be so many of them. After the time spent conversing, I learned that the venison steak that I had brought for our dinner that night had spoiled during the long, hot day. Elaine had told me that one small ice block was not enough to keep the meat warm—bring two large ice blocks she suggested. I ignored her advice and the result was a meatless dinner.

Below the campsite lies more superlative smallmouth cover, much like that already described except for three islets that dot the river. Be sure to weave in and out among these small land masses as the fishing is often exceptional here. This is also a great place to go bird watching, and hearken to the orchard orioles, wood thrushes, and red-eyed vireos that dwell on river left.

Not long after you pass Mason Island, you will come to Whites Ferry after about 20 minutes of paddling—the water moves fairly slowly through here. Here you can watch motorists being ferried across the Potomac River at Whites Ferry.

35

WHITES FERRY TO EDWARDS FERRY

U.S.G.S. QUADS:
Poolesville, Waterford Leesburg, Sterling

DISTANCE:
5 miles

RAPIDS:
Riffles

ACCESS POINTS:
At Whites Ferry (Montgomery County, MD), there is a concrete ramp on river left off Whites Ferry Road via MD Route 28. Parking spaces are numerous in a large lot. Note: this is fee parking. At Edwards Ferry (Montgomery County, MD), there is a concrete ramp on river left off Edwards Ferry Road via Westerly Road. Parking spaces are numerous in a paved lot.

O N JULY 17, 1991, Elaine and I fished the Potomac with guide Ken Penrod in the Whites Ferry area. Elaine and I each caught five smallmouths over a foot. She caught all of hers on mad toms; I caught mine on mad toms and Mister Twister Phenom worms. Obviously, lo these many years later, there is no way that I could remember that day in such detail—except for the comprehensive fishing records I have kept for many decades. In my fishing log notebook, I record the date, time, river, trip, weather and water conditions of every outing. Also recorded are the lures and flies that enticed every smallmouth over a foot, what

One of the best landmarks on the entire Main Stem is Whites Ferry.

time the fish was landed, how many smallies over a foot were lost, how many smallies under a foot were caught, plus how many fish of other species were caught. These detailed records help me write my magazine articles and books with more accuracy. But, just as importantly, these records help me do better on later trips because they give me baseline data of what previously worked. Granted the patterns that performed well on one trip may be totally ineffective the next time, but they at least provide a starting point.

Whites Ferry is the only operating ferry on the entire Potomac, so be sure to take some pictures of this little bit of Americana. But be aware of the cable that extends across the river and obviously do not interfere with this business. I have taken this float a number of times and have found the action mediocre at best near the ferry. About a mile downstream, though, some fantastic fishing begins. Several islets dot the river above Harrison Island, which extends downstream for a little over 2 miles.

Although the left side offers deeper water, I prefer scooting down the narrower right side to fish the several islets that concentrate fish as well as the good habitat: boulder field followed by submerged rocky cover, another island, and water willow and elodea throughout. About halfway down Harrison Island, you'll come to Balls Bluff on river right. The steep hillside and the rocks below it seem to concentrate the bass. Interestingly, I've caught channel cats along this island while fishing for smallies.

More rock bluffs below Harrison Island help mark a rocky shoreline that can provide good fishing. The river flows over scattered submerged rocky cover for the final 1½ miles of this float. Though these areas can fish well, they pale in comparison to the fishing upstream—be sure to budget your fishing time accordingly. Goose Creek enters the river on the right bank, across from the Edwards Ferry ramp on river left.

36

EDWARDS FERRY TO ALGONKIAN PARK

U.S.G.S. QUADS:
Sterling, Seneca

DISTANCE:
6 miles

RAPIDS:
Riffles

ACCESS POINTS:
At Edwards Ferry (Montgomery County, MD), there is a concrete ramp on river left off Edwards Ferry Road via Westerly Road. Parking spaces are numerous in a paved lot. At Algonkian Park (Loudoun County, VA), there is a river right paved ramp off Potomac View Road via Route 7. Parking spaces are numerous.

THE EDWARDS FERRY float is an interesting one that allows anglers and paddlers to explore a variety of habitats. Tyler Frankenberry of River Riders likes to fish a series of rocky habitats, water willow and star grass patches, lay downs, and small riffles that are scattered throughout the first mile of the excursion on river left. Indeed, on one trip, my first cast of the day was greeted with a thunderous strike of a muskie that had found a downed sycamore as the perfect lair. This type of habitat, says Frankenberry, is ideal for run-and-gun fishing—making quick casts then moving on down the river to the next likely spot.

Tyler Frankenberry with a nice smallmouth he caught on the Edwards Ferry float.

After mile 1, expect to see the star grass become even denser, especially as summer waxes and the water temperature becomes warmer. Star grass is an interesting native, aquatic grass that is best identified by its small yellow flowers shaped like stars. This vegetation typically grows in bottoms characterized by sand or small pebbles and water less than five feet deep. In shallower liquid, the grass forms massive mats that can slow a boat as you try to slide across it and makes navigation frustrating.

One of the best things about star grass is that it serves as a giant nursery for young of the year smallmouth bass, rock bass, redbreast sunfish, and other game fish. There they prey on each other and various aquatic insects and small minnows. If the grass does not become matted and there are small sections of open water in between the clumps, you can have good fishing, especially under low light conditions. That's a good time for fly fishermen to cast poppers to the openings and for spin fishermen to throw top-waters, especially buzzbaits. On one excursion through here, I met a local angler who told me he had spent 7½ hours fruitlessly working a vast star grass field, then the smallies turned on and he caught three nice ones in 30 minutes—a common experience with this type of cover.

Selden Island is barely distinguishable from the river right shoreline until you come to the end of it just past mile 3. Then you will come to a large gap between Selden and the next island, Van Deventer, which is part of the McKee Beshers Wildlife Management Area (WMA). You can paddle down the left side of Van Deventer, and pleasure boaters might want to do so, but anglers might want to enter the riffle-filled gap and fish the passage between the WMA and river right. The upper half of this passageway boasts exceptional smallmouth habitat says Frankenberry, and I agree. This is a great locale to work streamers and crankbaits as you drift along with the current. For example, on one trip, I caught a fine smallie that slammed a Big O and catapulted into the heavens three separate times. The bottom half of the passageway has good habitat but the current slows. As is just about always true on the Potomac, be sure to fish the tip of this island.

When you pass the tip, you will have traveled just over 5 miles and immediately arrive at a short, narrow island with the interesting name of Tenfoot. Both paddlers and anglers should stay to the right of this island and the latter should probe the odd riffle and underwater rocks. Half way past Tenfoot Island and before you come to the next island, Sharpshin, you will arrive at the river right take-out at Algonkian Regional Park.

37

ALGONKIAN PARK TO SENECA

U.S.G.S. QUADS:
Sterling, Seneca
DISTANCE:
2 miles
RAPIDS:
Riffles
ACCESS POINTS:
At Algonkian Park (Loudoun County, VA), a river right concrete ramp off Potomac View Road via Route 7 provides access with numerous parking spaces. At Seneca (Montgomery County, MD), there is a concrete ramp on river left off Rileys Lock Road via River Road with plenty of parking in a gravel lot. You will have to paddle up Seneca Creek a short distance to reach the access point.

THE SHORT FLOAT from Algonkian Regional Park to Seneca Creek is one of my least favorites on the Main Stem, and fishermen will likely only want to take it if they prefer to put in at the park instead of traveling to Maryland to access the river at the Seneca Creek launch. On the other hand, canoeists and kayakers, especially if they just want a short interlude on the water with their children, will find this float a pleasant way to spend a few hours afloat with kids in tow. No rapids exist, and this is a safe float for youngsters to become introduced to paddling. Birders may also like this float as bald eagles,

Seneca Aqueduct, near Poolesville, Maryland, USA. Built in 1833 to bring the C&O Canal over Seneca Creek. Riley's Lockhouse at upper right. Mary Ann Daly photo

ospreys, great blue and green herons, belted kingfishers, and assorted songbirds are common.

In fact, on one float through here, I witnessed a bombastic battle between a belted kingfisher and green heron. Normally, separate bird species live in relative harmony unless a bird of prey, think hawk, appears and then the various songbirds will sound their various alarm notes. Another example is when a crow comes close to a songbird's nest and the male may attempt to chase away its much larger adversary. Most conflicts, however, occur between males of the same species, which are trying to protect both their turf and mates. Male birds sing not because they are happy as many people think, but because they are warning other males of their species to stay out of their territory.

Anyway in the aforementioned skirmish between the belted kingfisher and green heron, I could not tell which of the two had invaded the other's section of the river. But much squalling and chasing took place, threats were issued and reissued, and then a temporary cease-fire was arranged. I moved on down the river, and the two species resumed their never-ending quest to gulp down small fish.

The river left side of this float is characterized by a woody shoreline, which is part of the Seneca Creek State Park. This shoreline has the best cover (the scattered downed tree or patch of aquatic vegetation) but the river flows slowly and during the summer especially, smallmouth activity is sporadic. The right bank, for the most part after you pass the park and where Sugarland Run enters on river right, has a barren shoreline. A golf course lies along the river right bank from about the ¾-mile point to the end of the float. Someone or entity in their foolishness has eliminated the entire tree line on this bank, giving the golfers "a great view of the river" to their way of thinking but created an eyesore and erosion. In the summer, vast star grass fields lie baking in the heat.

Near the 1¾ mile point, you'll note a dock, a large concrete water intake structure, and a flag pole. Beyond that lies the remains of Dam No. 2. If you are taking out at Seneca Creek on river left, as soon as you spot the creek's aqueduct, paddle over to it and then go upstream to the access point.

38

SENECA TO RIVERBEND PARK

U.S.G.S. QUAD:
Seneca

DISTANCE:
7 miles

RAPIDS:
Riffles, Class Is, and Class IIs. Class I-III rock garden (known as Seneca Breaks) below Dam No. 2.

ACCESS POINTS:
At Seneca (Montgomery County, MD), there is a concrete ramp on river left off Rileys Lock Road via River Road. Parking spaces are numerous in a gravel lot. You will have to paddle down Seneca Creek a short distance to reach the river. At Riverbend Park (Fairfax County, VA), there is a steep, river right concrete ramp off Potomac Hill Street via Jeffrey Road. Parking spaces are numerous in a paved lot.

AFTER YOU LAUNCH, paddle immediately to the far river right shoreline. Do not attempt to run the remains of Dam No. 2. On far river right, you will see a narrow approximately one-mile long passageway known as the Virginia Canal. Tyler Frankenberry of River Riders recommends that anglers and paddlers take this route rather than running the Class I-III rock garden below the dam. On my excursion with Tyler, we encountered a number of Class I and II rapids in the creek-like environs of the Virginia Canal. These rapids can turn

A view of the Virginia Canal on the Seneca float.

into Class IIIs in high water. Whether you run Seneca Breaks or the Virginia Canal, you should be an expert paddler.

Tyler recommends that anglers and paddlers negotiating the Virginia Canal hug the river right side until they come to Patowmack Island, a little over a mile from the dam. Afterwards through the end of the trip, the Potomac flows at a fast clip but there are no major rapids. And the fishing and scenery are simply outstanding. Below Patowmack comes Elm Island and good spots for smallmouth on both sides. The swift water is ideal for spin enthusiasts who like to throw spinnerbaits (Tyler's choice) or long rodders who like to cast streamers.

The next major feature is three-mile-long Watkins Island. Katie Island lies at its upper end and Grapevine Island to Watkins' right. Again, all of this cover on all sides is replete with riffles, runs, underwater rocks, and elodea and water willow beds. After you pass Grapevine Island, you will come to a series of islets between Watkins and the river right shoreline. Numerous boils pock the water throughout and the fishing remains excellent. This, too, is a scenic area and a nice place to stop and take pictures.

After you have been traveling down Watkins Island for about 1½

The Great Falls below Riverbend Acess. You don't want to miss your takeout!

miles, you will come to Clagett Island. To the right of that island lies a rocky bank along river right that provides good fishing. Watkins Island finally ends about 5 miles below the dam, but it is hard to determine so because Gladys Island lies immediately next to it.

You now have about ¾ of a mile left in the float, and I strongly suggest that you hug the river right shoreline throughout. Downstream lies Great Falls, one of the most dangerous areas on any Mid-Atlantic river with Class IV-plus rapids. You don't want to miss your take-out and have to contend with Great Falls or paddle upstream.

Beyond Gladys Island is the Minnehaha Island area and the numerous islets that lie close to it. More superlative smallmouth action is possible here as the riffles and mid-river rock cover harbor fish. You will then come around a short river right bend and arrive at the Riverbend access point.

39

MAPS

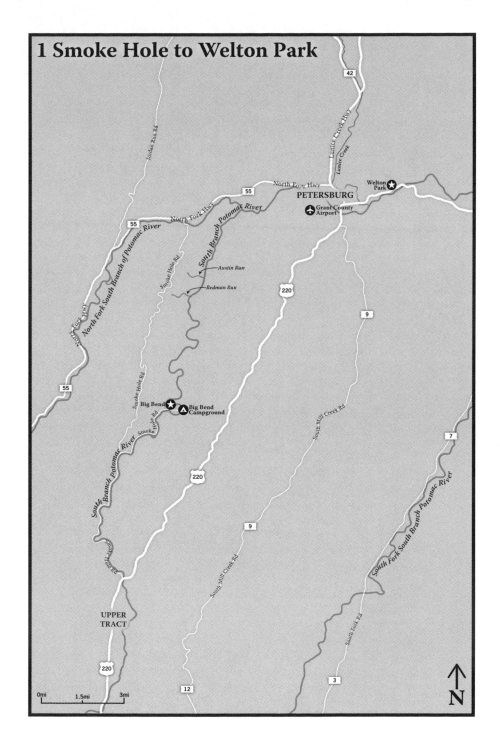

1 Smoke Hole to Welton Park

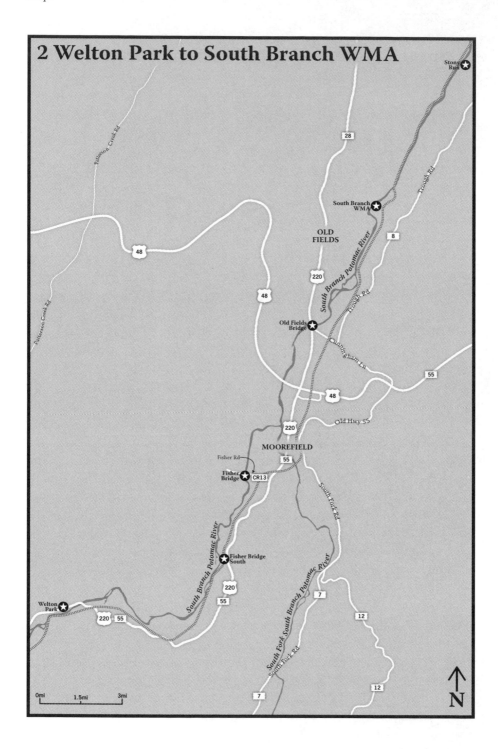

2 Welton Park to South Branch WMA

Stony Run

28

Trough Rd

South Branch WMA

48

Patterson Creek Rd

OLD FIELDS

South Branch Potomac River

8

220

48

Trough Rd

Patterson Creek Rd

Old Fields Bridge

Cunningham Ln

55

48

Old Hwy 55

220

MOOREFIELD

Fisher Rd

55

Fisher Bridge CR13

South Fork Rd

South Branch Potomac River

Fisher Bridge South

South Fork South Branch Potomac River

220

55

7

Welton Park

220 55

12

South Fork Rd

7

12

0mi   1.5mi   3mi

N

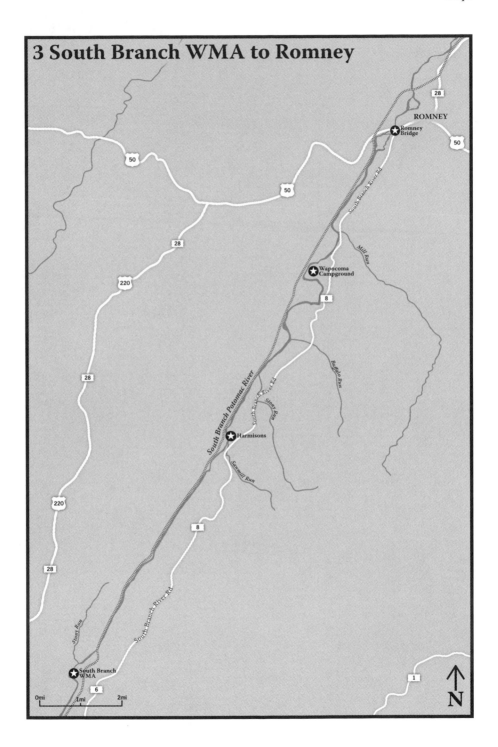

3 South Branch WMA to Romney

ROMNEY

Romney Bridge

28

50

50

50

South Branch River Rd

Mill Run

Wapocoma Campground

8

28

220

Buffalo Run

South Branch Potomac River

28

South Branch River Rd

Stony Run

Harmisons

Sawmill Run

220

8

28

Stuart Run

South Branch River Rd

South Branch WMA

6

1

0mi   1mi   2mi

N

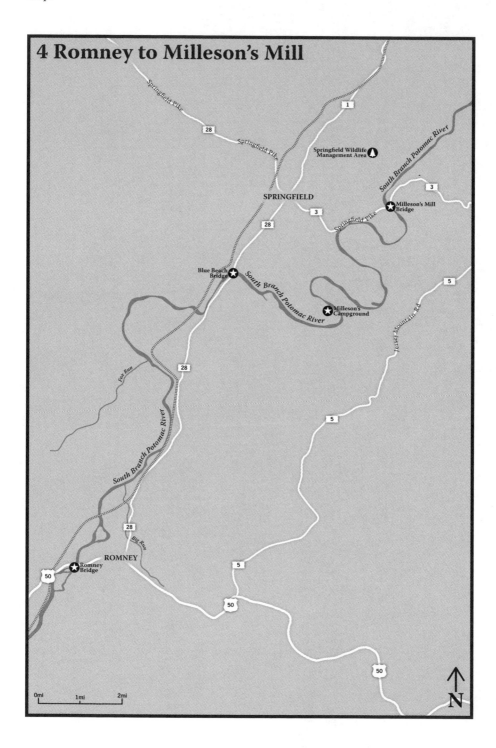

4 Romney to Milleson's Mill

Springfield Pike

28

Springfield Pike

1

Springfield Wildlife
Management Area

South Branch Potomac River

SPRINGFIELD

3

Milleson's Mill
Bridge

3

28

Springfield Pike

Blue Beach
Bridge

South Branch Potomac River

5

Milleson's
Campground

Jersey Mountain Rd.

Fox Run

28

5

South Branch Potomac River

28

Big Run

ROMNEY

5

Romney
Bridge

50

50

50

0mi   1mi   2mi

N

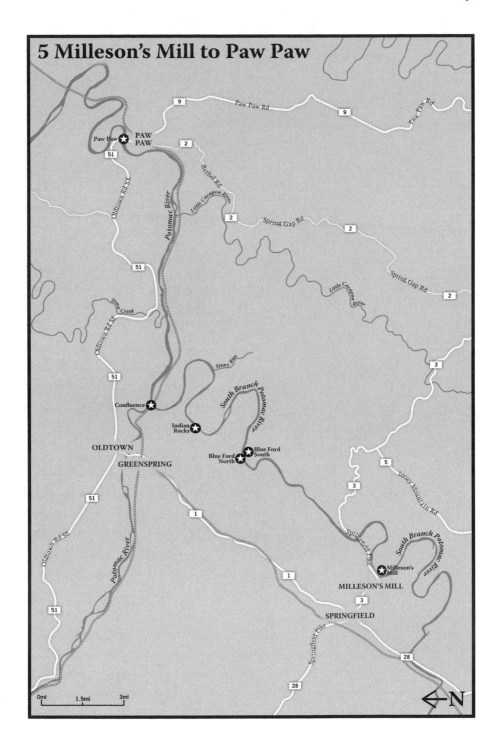

5 Milleson's Mill to Paw Paw

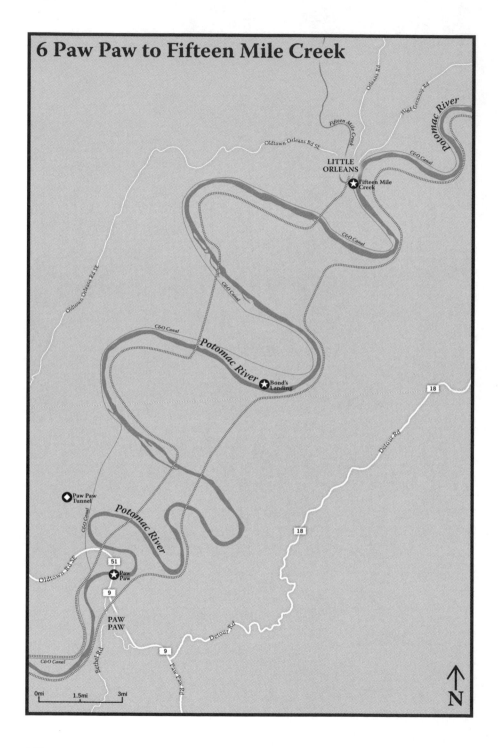

6 Paw Paw to Fifteen Mile Creek

7 Fifteen Mile Creek to Hancock

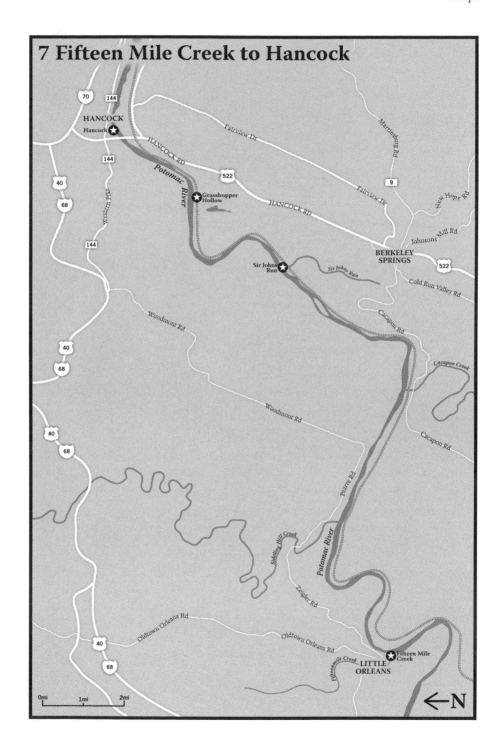

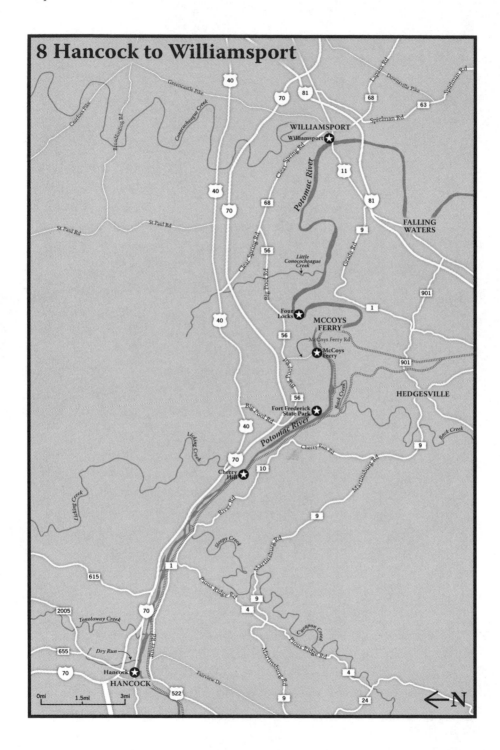

8 Hancock to Williamsport

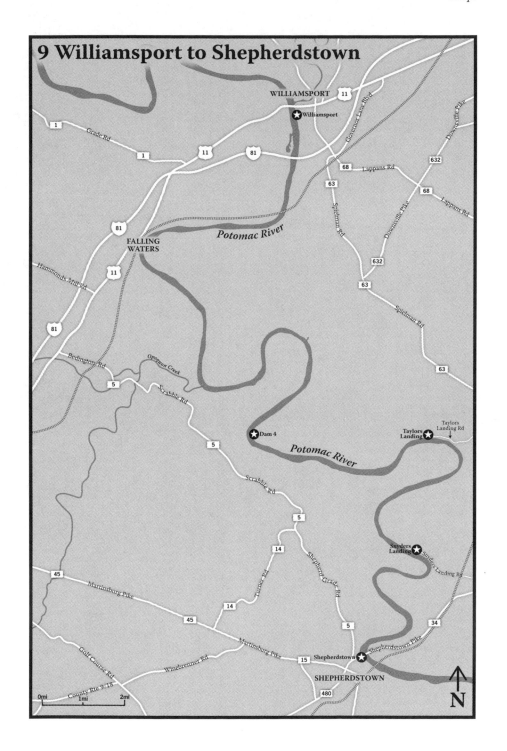

9 Williamsport to Shepherdstown

WILLIAMSPORT · 11

Williamsport

Grade Rd · 1

1

11

81

Governor Lane Blvd

68 · Lappans Rd

632

63

Downsville Pike

68 · Lappans Rd

Spielman Rd

Downsville Pike

81

FALLING WATERS

Potomac River

632

63

11

Hammonds Mill Rd

Spielman Rd

81

Bedington Rd

Opequon Creek

63

Scrabble Rd

5

Dam 4

Taylors Landing Rd

5

Potomac River

Taylors Landing

Scrabble Rd

5

14

Snyders Landing

45

Martinsburg Pike

Shepherds Grade Rd

Snyders Landing Rd

14

45

5

34

Martinsburg Pike

Golf Course Rd

Winebrenner Rd

15

Shepherdstown

Shepherdstown Pike

SHEPHERDSTOWN

County Rte 9/18

480

0mi 1mi 2mi

N

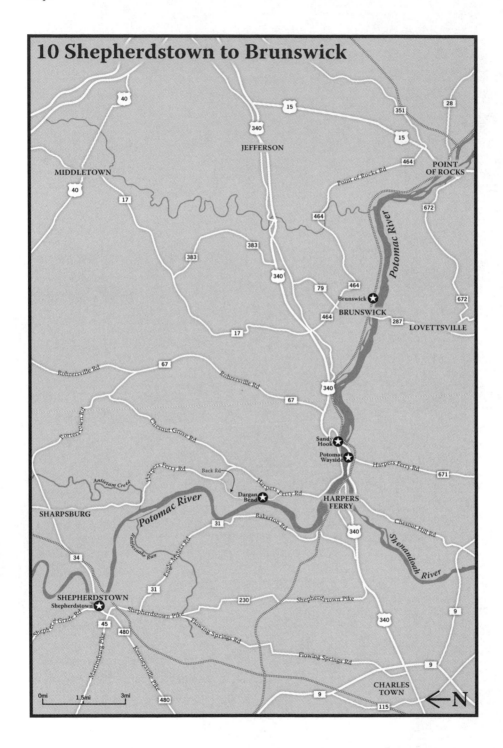

10 Shepherdstown to Brunswick

JEFFERSON

MIDDLETOWN

Point of Rocks Rd

POINT
OF ROCKS

Potomac River

BRUNSWICK

LOVETTSVILLE

Rohrersville Rd

Rohrersville Rd

Chesnut Grove Rd

Porters own Rd

Harpers Ferry Rd

Back Rd

Harpers Ferry Rd

Harpers Ferry Rd

Antietam Creek

Dargan
Bend

Sandy
Hook

Potomac
Wayside

HARPERS
FERRY

SHARPSBURG

Potomac River

Bakerton Rd

Chesnut Hill Rd

Shenandoah River

Nationale Run

Eagle Meyhres Rd

SHEPHERDSTOWN
Shepherdstown

Shepherd Grade Rd

Shepherdstown Pike

Shepherdstown Pike

Flowing Springs Rd

Flowing Springs Rd

Martinsburg Pike

Kearneysville Pike

CHARLES
TOWN

0mi   1.5mi   3mi

← N

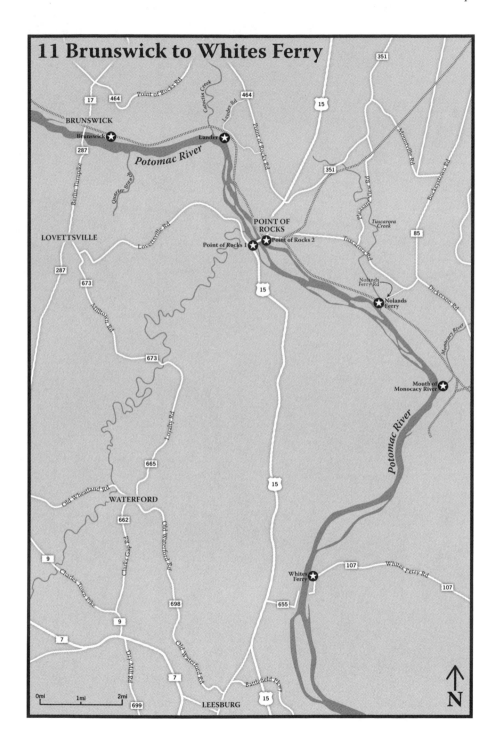

11 Brunswick to Whites Ferry

351

Point of Rocks Rd

Catoctin Creek

17   464   Lander Rd   464

BRUNSWICK   15

Lander

Point of Rocks Rd

Montville Rd

Buckeystown Rd

Brunswick   Lander

287   *Potomac River*

351

Berlin Turnpike

Quarter Branch

Pleasant Rd

Tuscarora Creek

85

POINT OF ROCKS

Tuscarora Rd

LOVETTSVILLE   Lovettsville Rd   Point of Rocks 1   Point of Rocks 2

287

673

Nolands Ferry Rd

Dickerson Rd

15

Nolands Ferry

Milltown Rd

Monocacy River

673

Mouth of Monocacy River

665

Potomac River

Old Wheatland Rd   **WATERFORD**   15

662

Old Waterford Rd

Clarke Gap Rd

Pig Spring Rd

9

Charles Town Pike

Whites Ferry   107   Whites Ferry Rd

698   Whites Ferry   107

9   655

7

Dry Mill Rd

Old Waterford Rd

Battlefield Pkwy

0mi   1mi   2mi   7

699   **LEESBURG**   15

N

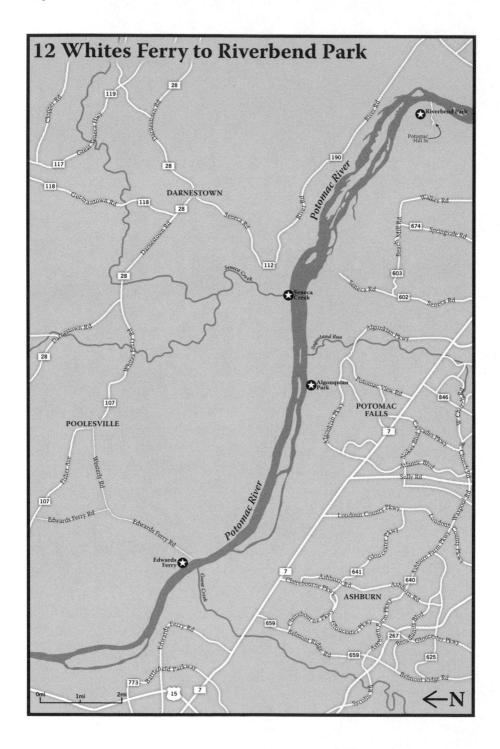

12 Whites Ferry to Riverbend Park

40

RESOURCES

MAPS AND ACCESS INFORMATION

C&O National Historical Park
(301) 739-4200, www.nps.gov/choh
Great for information on where campsites are located along the Main Stem.

Virginia Atlas & Gazetteer, West Virginia Atlas & Gazetteer, and
Maryland and Delaware Atlas & Gazetteer
are essential for traversing back roads, available from DeLorme,
(800) 561-5105, www.delorme.com

MyTopo, www.mytopo.com
The program I used for navigating rivers is Terrain Navigator Pro.

Maryland Boat Ramps
www.dnr.maryland.gov/boating/boatramps.asp

West Virginia
www.wvdnr.gov/fishing/public_access.asp?county=all&type=River
%2Bfloattrips

FISHING LICENSES AND REGULATIONS

Maryland Department of Natural Resources
www.dnr.state.md.us

Virginia Department of Game and Inland Fisheries
www.dgif.virginia.gov

West Virginia Division of Natural Resources
www.wvdnr.gov

OUTFITTERS

I have personally fished with these outfitters and can recommend them.

James Apperson
(304) 724-7373
www.bassriveroutfitters.com

Eagle's Nest Outfitters
Petersburg, West Virginia
(304) 257-2393, www.eaglesnestoutfitters.com
Canoe rentals, shuttles, guided trips.

Ken Pavol (North Branch Angler)
kenpavol@pennswoods.net
(240) 321-1495 or (301) 387-5314
Guides only for trout.

Ken Penrod (Life Outdoors Unlimited)
(301) 937-0010, www.penrodsguides.com

River Riders
Harpers Ferry, West Virginia
(304) 535-2663 or (800) 326 7238
www.riverriders.com

ADDITIONAL OUTFITTERS

River & Trail Outfitters
Knoxville, Maryland
(301) 695-5177, (888-) i-go-play
www.rivertrail.com

Tom's Run Outfitters
Hagerstown, Maryland
(301) 733-0058
www.tomsrunoutfitters.com

ORGANIZATIONS

Potomac River Smallmouth Club
www.prsc.org

Potomac Riverkeeper
www.potomacriverkeeper.org

Shenandoah Riverkeeper
www.shenandoahriverkeeper.org

Virginia Outdoors Foundation
www.virginiaoutdoorsfoundation.org

CAMPING

West Virginia Campgrounds and State Parks

Milleson's Walnut Grove Campground
(304) 822-5284, www.millesonscampground.com

Wapocoma Family Campground
(304) 822-5528, www.wapocomocampground.com

Berkeley Springs State Park
(800) CALL-WVA, berkeleyspringssp.com

Cacapon Resort State Park
(800) CALL-WVA, cacaponresort.com

MARYLAND

TOURISM RESOURCES

Maryland Office of Tourism
(410) 767-3400; (800) 719-5900
www.visitmaryland.org

Garrett County Chamber of Commerce
(301) 387-4386
www.visitdeepcreek.com

Allegany County Tourism
(800) 425-2067
www.mdmountainside.com

Hagerstown-Washington County CVB
(301) 791-3246; (888) 257-2600
www.marylandmemories.com

Tourism Council of Frederick County, Inc.
(301) 600-2888; (800) 999-3613
www.fredericktourism.org

CVB of Montgomery, MD, Inc.
(240) 777-2060; (877) 789-6904
www.visitmontgomery.com

BED AND BREAKFASTS (B&BS)

I want to explain my listing of so many bed and breakfasts. While I was researching this book, Elaine and I spent one night at Stone Manor Vineyard and Orchard Bed & Breakfast. I was too exhausted from floating the Potomac that evening to converse with owner Spencer Ault, but the next morning over breakfast three of us had a grand time talking about the Potomac River and the history of his inn and area. Staying at a B&B and meeting folks like Spencer can really enhance the experience of floating the Potomac or any waterway.

Canal Quarters
The National Park Service operates Canal Quarters in conjunction with a trust where visitors can stay overnight in lock houses along the C&O Canal. Styles, amenities and other options vary, www.canaltrust.org/quarters.

1828 Trail Inn Bed & Breakfast
Hancock, MD 21750
(301) 678-7227
www.1828-trail-inn.com

Antietam's Jacob Rohrbach Inn B&B
Sharpsburg, MD 21782
(301) 432-5079
www.jacob-rohrbach-inn.com

Bruce House Inn
Cumberland, MD 21502
1-(866-) 777-8181, (301) 777-8860
www.brucehouseinn.com

Inn at Antietam
Sharpsburg, MD 21782
(301) 432-6601; (877-) 835-6011
www.innatantietam.com

Inn on Decatur
Cumberland, MD 21502
(301) 722-4887; (800) 459-0510
www.theinnondecatur.net

Pleasant Springs Farm Bed and Breakfast
Boyd, MD 20841
(301) 972-3452
www.pleasantspringsfarm.com

Riverrun B&B
Hancock, MD 21750
(301) 678-6150
www.riverrunbnb.com

River's Edge Farm
  Oldtown, MD 21555
  (301) 478-5424
  www.barbsalpacas.com

Town Hill B&B
  Little Orleans, MD 21766
  (301) 478-2794, (877) 696-2794
  www.townhillbnb.com

VIRGINIA

TOURISM RESOURCES

Loudoun County Visitors Center
  112-G South St., SE
  Leesburg, VA 20175
  (800) 752-6118 or (703) 771-2170
  www.visitloudoun.org

Highland County Chamber of Commerce
  (540) 468-2550
  www.highlandcounty.org

BED AND BREAKFASTS (B&BS)

The Highland Inn
  (540) 468-2143 or (888) 466-3143
  www.highland-inn.com

Loudoun County B&B
  Stone Manor Vineyard and Orchard Bed & Breakfast
  Lovettsville, Virginia 20180
  (540) 822-3032
  www.mycountryretreat.com

WEST VIRGINIA

TOURISM RESOURCES

West Virginia Division of Tourism
90 MacCorkle Ave., SW
South Charleston, WV 25303
(800) CALL-WVA
www.wvtourism.com

Berkeley Springs (Morgan County)
127 Fairfax Street
Berkeley Springs WV 25411
(800) 447-8797
tbs@berkeleysprings.com
www.berkeleysprings.com

Grant County CVB
126 S. Main Street
Petersburg, WV 26847
(304) 257-9266
grantcountycvb@frontiernet.net
www.grantcountywva.com

Hampshire County Visitors Bureau
426 E. Main Street
Romney, WV 26557
(304) 822-7477
hampshirevisitorsbureau@citlink.net
www.cometohampshire.com

Hardy County Tourism
P.O. Box 797
Moorefield, WV 26826
(304) 897-8700
info@visithardy.com
www.visithardy.com

Jefferson County CVB
37 Washington Court
Harpers Ferry, WV 25425
(866) HELLO-WV
execdir@wveasterngateway.com
www.wveasterngateway.com

Pendleton County Tourism
P.O. Box 737
Franklin, WV 26807
(304) 358-3884
pendletoncoc@frontier.net
www.visitpendleton.com

Ranson Tourism (Jefferson County)
312 S. Mildred St.
Ranson, WV 25438
(304) 724-3862
cmills@cityofransonwv.net
www.cityofransonwv.net

Shepherdstown Visitors Center (Jefferson County)
P.O. Box 329
Shepherdstown, WV 25433
(304) 876-2786
www.shepherdstownvisitorscenter.com

BED AND BREAKFASTS (B&BS)

Asa Cline House
Yellow Spring, WV
(304) 874-4115 or (866) 665-4115
www.asaclinehouse.com

Breath of Heaven B&B
Petersburg, WV
(304) 257-4971
www.breathofheavenbb.com

Country Inn at High View
High View, WV
(304) 856-1415
www.thecountryinnathighview.com

North Fork Mountain Inn
Cabins, WV
(304) 668-4918
www.northforkmtninn.com

Silver Maple Hubbard Inn
Franklin, WV
(304) 902-9007
www.hubbardsinn.com

The Inn at Lost River
Lost River, WV
(304) 897-7000
www.theinnatlostriver.com

Carriage Inn B&B
Charles Town, WV
(304) 728-8003 or (800) 867-9830
www.carriageinn.com

Harpers Ferry Guest House
Harpers Ferry, WV
(304) 535-2101
www.harpersferryguesthouse.com

Laurel Lodge
Harpers Ferry, WV
(304) 535-2886
www.laurellodge.com

Maria's Garden
Berkeley Springs, WV
(304) 258-2021 or (888) 629-2253
www.mariasgarden.com

The Manor Inn
(304) 258-1552 or (800) 974-5770
Berkeley Springs, WV
www.bathmanorinn.com

Sleepy Creek Mountain Inn
Berkeley Springs, WV
(304) 258-0234 or (877) 258-0234
www.sleepycreekmountaininn.com

The Jackson Rose B&B
Harpers Ferry, WV
(304) 535-1528
www.thejacksonrose.com

The Town's Inn
Harpers Ferry, WV
(877) 489-2447
www.thetownsinn.com

Thomas Shepherd Inn
Shepherdstown, WV
(304) 876-3715 or (888) 889-8952
www.thomasshepherdinn.com